The Restoration of Politics

*For Bob
affectionately
George*

The Restoration of Politics

*Interrogating History
about a Civilization in Crisis*

George Liska

ROWMAN & LITTLEFIELD PUBLISHERS, INC.

ROWMAN & LITTLEFIELD PUBLISHERS, INC.

Published in the United States of America
by Rowman & Littlefield Publishers, Inc.
4720 Boston Way, Lanham, Maryland 20706

3 Henrietta Steet
London WC2E 8LU, England

Copyright © 1996 by Rowman & Littlefield Publishers, Inc.

All rights reserved. No part of this publication may be reproduced,
stored in a retrieval system, or transmitted in any form or by any
means, electronic, mechanical, photocopying, recording, or otherwise,
without the prior permission of the publisher.

British Cataloging in Publication Information Available

Library of Congress Cataloging-in-Publication Data
Liska, George.
The restoration of politics : interrogating history about a
civilization in crisis / by George Liska.
p.   cm.
Includes bibliographical references.
1. United States—Foreign relations—1989–   I. Title.
E881.L57   1996   327.73—dc20   95-52539   CIP

ISBN 0-8476-8212-9 (cloth : alk. paper)
ISBN 0-8476-8213-7 (pbk. : alk. paper)

Printed in the United States of America

∞™ The paper used in this publication meets the minimum requirements of
American National Standard for Information Sciences—Permanence of
Paper for Printed Library Materials, ANSI Z39.48—1984.

Contents

Author's Prefatory Note	vii
Introduction. A Revolution for American Byzantium	1
Discourse I. About Past and Present: Salient Challenges and Particular Responses	9
Interrogation I. A Civil War: Symptom or Emblem?	23
Discourse II. About the Two Cities of Man: Insecure Prosperity and Rebelling Poverty	33
Interrogation II. A Crisis: Global or National?	47
Discourse III. About Principles and Practice: Imperfect Politics and Grand Strategy	53
Interrogation III. A Contract: With Self or the World?	69
Discourse IV. From Present to Future: Predicaments and Prophecy	77
Interrogation IV. A Civilization: Atlanticist or Euro-American?	93
Conclusion: Historicist Intuition versus Postmodern Revolutions	101
Notes	125
Index	127
About the Author	133

Author's Prefatory Note

In view of what follows, it may be useful to state at the outset that I am not, nor have I ever been, an isolationist. As possibilities and necessities changed, I have successively argued for an American empire and a U.S.-Soviet condominium, both needful of substantial American engagement in the world and political maturity at home.[1] My being isolated in both of the propositions from official policymakers as well as academic brethren does not prove in the face of already transpired and yet to be feared consequences of contrary policies that my propositions were altogether wrong and my pleas hopelessly wrongheaded. Nor does it prove that the same weakness befalls what I now believe to be the logical implication and practical result of neither of the exacting engagements materializing.

Least of all is the argument for intelligent American retrenchment abroad for the sake of internal recovery automatically anti-American because it is made by an old-fashioned European of the generically continentalist (i.e., currently "gaullist") persuasion. As the Cold War unfolded, it was in fact a distinguished Briton who warned this nation against the "illusion of omnipotence," while a not less prominent American indicted its leaders of the "arrogance of power." Both the recommendation and the rebuke become pathetically more urgent when the power or the will to use it is markedly less. Illusion becomes then wholly delusionary while arrogance changes into mere pretense before degenerating into petulance. This risk is run by an America that, while rightly focusing its available energies on a multifaceted crisis within, consigns leadership abroad to an inflated rhetoric by the nation's leaders and intermittent tours de force of its diplomats.

A cardinal question arises inevitably in a wider and longer historical perspective: Will America's sheer existence prove in the end to have been a good thing for the world, or, at least, a neutrally indifferent matter when the sum of determining deeds and events, including the now-occurring, will be in hand? Or else is what I will later refer to as this republic's phantom hegemony shot through with equally watered down hubris in ways customary for successful insular-oceanic polities when they assert an also morally tone-setting influence vis-à-vis more directly embattled and situationally less favored continental powers? Only one thing is certain: The customary blending of hegemony and hubris is at its morally as well as politically most problematic when the expectations and dependencies it encourages in others are finally shown to have been mistaken.

What follows is devoted to grappling with this query, a more authoritative answer to which will continue to be written by the deeds that will fill the final pages of the record left behind for adjudication by the American Century.

The idea for this book grew out of a lecture on the perennial themes of Russia and Europe offered as a response to my colleague and fellow-Slav Zbigniew Brzezinski's different views on the subject, put forward at the Nitze School of Advanced International Studies of the Johns Hopkins University on the occasion of the fiftieth anniversary of Yalta. The book's main theses were subsequently presented to the Johns Hopkins Foreign Policy Institute as part of an exploration of U.S. foreign policy alternatives presided over by Dean Paul Wolfowitz and organized by Andrew Bacevich. It will not take long for the reader to discover that, much as I may have profited from criticisms, not the slightest guilt by association can attach to attendance at one of these events or participation in the other.

Disguised as a memorandum for the policymaker defying the orthodoxies of the age, this highly personal memoir is less a work of diligent scholarship than a stream-of-consciousness meditation following intertwining strands of reality and reflection almost at random. In order to conform to the book's main theme and bring some order into chaos, a long essay is divided into four discourses, each of which presents a historical background for an interrogation framed in terms of two alternatives, to which the preferred answer is the reconciliation of artificial opposites in a forward movement toward a future that is less stressful but no less creative than the past.

Introduction
A Revolution for American Byzantium?

As this little book goes to press, a great debate about America's role in the post-Cold War world is at long last taking off. In keeping with the current scale of world politics, the discussion revolves around a relatively minor issue—the role of the U.S. military in helping enforce peace in a faraway small country in the Balkans, about which we know virtually nothing but pretend to know much.

Should the United States dispatch a military contingent to Bosnia or not; rearm the local Muslims so as to buttress a fragile peace settlement in the long run while undermining the chances for its peaceful implementation from the start; do the rearming openly and thus maximize the risk or semi-clandestinely through surrogates? That is to say, should this country act unilaterally or vouchsafe another chance to a species of multilateralism that, upgraded militarily, has become more muscular than its unmanageable UN predecessor? In one style or the other, should America behave (at long last?) as a true great power by matching available means with a carefully limited but sternly pursued objective, or act instead as an empire for the times that runs a messy world by means of correspondingly untidy and artfully ambiguous policies (because a full twenty years after forfeiting the chance to implement a genuine mandate for imperial order maintenance in more demanding but for the same reason more manageable circumstances)? Or, alternatively, should the United States leave alone what is already mending on its own and, confining NATO's mission to narrowly defined essentials, allow the local balance of military forces to subside on all sides and right itself spontaneously with help from economic asymmetries favoring the militarily weaker (i.e., Muslim) side? Doing so would avoid injecting new sources of aggravation into a psychological stalemate of contrary ambitions, recognized by all of the local parties to be beyond the reach of yet another violent endeavor. Finally, going still farther in the right direction, should America's GIs stay at home altogether and its government attend to the cure of the nation's ills rather than to the prevention of atrocities committed among others, and avoid thus confusing international politics with philanthropy?

Most of these arguments were rehearsed by prominent commentators in opinion pieces appearing in December 1995 over only two days in a single national newspaper.[2] Whatever may be the outcome of the debate and of the undertaking that gave rise to it, history's final judgment on America's more comprehensive performance will come from deeper down and depend on the direction taken by ambiguous present omens. Will America continue or will it arrest and even reverse its late sliding from the Augustan marriage of power with poetry in a Rome-like liberal empire, pledged at John F. Kennedy's inauguration, past the more prosaic Nixon-Kissinger effort to regenerate American power by redistributing the burdens attending its solitary employment? Will replacing this conservative effort to save what could be saved from liberal exuberance by movement toward a centrist and, therefore, practically nondescript posture of the present prove to have been an advance toward greater enlightenment or a return to a much more distant and anything but uplifting past?

Such a past comes back to life whenever the most prominent function of America in world affairs has become to proclaim *urbi et orbi* newly minted peace accords reached under more symbolic than substantial U.S. auspices. A calculated effort to dazzle the world (and a largely inattentive-to-indifferent national electorate) may blind some to realities. But it fails to impress either the city (standing for metropolitan and foreign initiates) or any potential adversary outside the gates. The reality is that the special effects of a diplomatic theater can make up but little for the absence of serious foreign policy; that Byzantium-like ceremonial stagecraft updated U.S.-style is no adequate substitute for either classic statecraft or effectively defensive siegecraft—i.e., for the performance of either early or late imperial Rome.

As part of a continuing declension from America's two limited imperial wars through good offices still backed by "strategic relationships" at Camp David to officious diplomacy at Dayton, Ohio, devoid of dependable strategic or domestic sponsorship, it may do to herd together unruly barbarians in a condition of near-captivity at a remote military base. But for them to receive there and subsequently obey a quasi-imperial peace ordinance from today's Byzantium rhymes poorly with the reluctance of a so-called new Rome to dispatch its legionnaires for the imperial decree's enforcement. At a time when America's leadership and, under its guidance, the authority of the West rests less on economic prowess and societal or cultural vibrancy than on military hardware, a query cannot be so easily sidestepped. On a scale extending from the interwar vote of late-imperial Britain's elite youth, gathered in the Oxford Union, not to fight for King and Country (and the decision's active repeal in due course) to the actual refusal by this elite's American counterpart to bear arms for their country at the real American empire's embattled height, how is one to assess that which is looming beyond this still-unfinished spectrum of allergies to the use of force: the reluctance of the average American citizen to expose the U.S. military to professional risks all too familiar to the least experienced of big-city rookies and accepted by big-forest fire fighters as a matter of course in formally peaceful civilian America?

Are we witnessing a progressively accelerated recoil from the barbaric habits of a regrettable past, an improving judgment as to the causes (or "national interests") worth fighting and dying for, or something more disturbing? Are we present at the decline of the West or at its high-noon maturity, insofar as the two can be distinguished? As we await an answer, we are unable to determine the extent to which the contemporary diplomatic theater is harmless entertainment or a clever publicity stunt, providing a necessary brief respite from the more difficult business of reforming a social order and revitalizing a civilization. It may be admitted as largely true that U.S. ubiquitous interference short of meaningful intervention has been in part a response to calls by other parties for American involvement as the indispensable component of otherwise unsolvable equations. However, this marriage of convenience is no longer the consummation of political romance that weds simple home-grown poetry to impressive world-bestriding power, but an opportunistic coupling of two sets of domestic political imperatives: world leadership for the American side, extraneous imposition of compromises that have become unavoidable for the warring sides. The myth of the urgent necessity is a substitute for actual exertion, prohibited internally; the urgings are so many alibis for domestically dangerous concessions by the belligerents and unpopular acts of commission or omission by secondary bystanders—most recently the ex-Yugoslavs when brought under control at long last because of their exhaustion, and the onetime great European powers reluctantly settling for token participation in the final formal acts while ultimately marginalized in all but name.

Deceiving the Americans into mistaking the self-regarding convenience of others for the entitlement of generous America is a benign misunderstanding as long as it does not generate more painful future disappointments. These may well be reserved for a later or different set of others, presently encouraged and for present reasons of their own willing to mistake a mere semblance of dependable American performance for its substance. Tragicomedy revolves around mistaken identities and mystifying intentions. It has a highly uncertain happy ending in a world politics that, projected against the gloomy backdrop of threatening social crisis at the Euro-American West and more savagely violent upheavals at its periphery, has on its conspicuous surface been assuming many of the characteristics of a farce. Can this lower kind of drama be redeemed by intermittent displays of relatively low-cost seriousness or will the very excess of some of them, say the magnitude of NATO's Bosnian peace enforcement, defeat their purpose? One way or another, a mixed picture succeeds now to the travesty of tragedy in the melodramatization of international relations that ushered the Cold War into its terminal twilight in the early stages of the so-called Reagan revolution.

It is reserved for our reading and uses of history to determine whether its record delineates a more dignified exit from confusions of facts and values than can be found through either farce or melodrama. A progressive dissipation of individual and group calamities in restored societal civility might then be positively allied with the reactivation of high foreign politics, this threatened repository of hopes for a redeeming balance between ancient virtues and immemorial vices exemplified in authentic tragedy. A presently uninspiring scenery will meanwhile be haunted by the ghost of once-vibrant internationalism, a somewhat discredited but still hard-to-defy adjunct of a creed now mainly responsible for "political correctness," this hysterical revenge of reformist liberalism for its eclipse as a governing political doctrine. Thus also the defeat of institutionalized Marxism coincides paradoxically with the triumph of economic determinism under the auspices of classic liberalism posing as an update of traditional conservatism.

What insights, we can now ask from a so far established vantage point, has a recent Conservative Manifesto injected into the understanding of the global side of the contemporary predicament? What directive for U.S. foreign policy have the manifesto's authors introduced into the shapeless medley of defunct or deformed doctrines and related practices? Supplying such insights and directives is an integral part of a revolution when its architects set out to do battle with the status quo—in the present case with the indigenous branch of the two ostensibly rival but actually cognate, liberal-reformist and revolutionary-socialist, modern utopias.

Compared to its revolutionary sweep and ambition in domestic matters, the national security clause of the Republican party's "Contract with America" is actually strikingly narrow and the little of its substance is correspondingly shallow. The foreign policy doctrine appears limited to upgrading conventional national defense and to downgrading the control of the United Nations over U.S. peacekeeping or -making troops, inevitably "placed in harm's way" by misfired humanitarian missions around the world. An attempt to revitalize national security does not so much reinvent global strategy as it simply echoes the conventional prejudices, parading as traditional virtues, of a still (or again?) parochially-minded society.

Despite occasional disclaimers, Americans have grown addicted to the always flattering and often profitable attributes of world leadership. They have yet to learn how either to shoulder or responsibly distribute the related burdens. They seem unwilling to pay, and their national leadership unable to convincingly justify, the price of global leadership when it rises sharply, as it did in the case of the war in Southeast Asia, or goes up even a mere trifle above the acceptable norm, should this prove to be the case in Southeastern Europe. Similarly, both the general public and politicians are at a loss over how to adjust the practice and priorities of that leadership when the world's need for guidance declines or changes, as it has despite occasional appearances to the contrary in the aftermath of the Cold War.

In the first two decades of what came to be called The American Century, America grasped prematurely for a world role from within a society unready for such responsibility—under either a conservative (Theodore Roosevelt) or a liberal (Woodrow Wilson) guise. A wide chasm between surging material power and conceptually stagnating polity was then to blame for the inconsistencies of America's only semiconscious contention with Germany over the succession to the British empire. It took the mutual reinforcement of American power and polity during and immediately after the Second World War, a reprise of the previously undecided contest for succession, to narrow the original disparity between American military capabilities and political maturity. The narrowing was short-lived, however, and the gap widened again when the desire to protect the wartime achievement by reforming society helped dissolve the polity's support for modern America's first—and so far last—self-dependent reach for the garlands of imperial power. This bid to garner, Athens-like, the ultimate reward of victory over alien autocracy could not but propel American democracy into a still unfinished search for a balance between a proper use of the nation's power abroad and government's sustainable role and function at home.

At the next crossroads in the journey toward discovering and then realizing this country's true potential, a deeper transvaluation of its world-role than the one proposed in the Republican contract cannot leave standing all the assumed truths about foreign policy pioneered by liberalism and eventually adopted by the internationalist wing of American conservatism, only to be exposed to radical isolationism in the aftermath of the Vietnam War. A society reassured by victory in a larger conflict can now undertake a less hysterical, but no less critical, revision of the internationalist creed and its many corollaries than it was able to do in the throes of a humiliating defeat. A crucial part of such revision is an update of America's otherwise imperceptibly, and thus all the more damagingly, expiring tacit understandings with the world. A more explicit contract is necessary because twentieth-century America's relationship with the world has until lately eschewed the measure of equality between parties necessary for a genuine compact. Equality applied least to America's role and status as a trustee of the post-World War II order, developing into an empire in all but name from the impetus of opposition to the order's challenger. Failure to recognize any polity's highest possible achievement for what it was and could have continued accomplishing undermined its further development and progressive institutionalization. Implementing equilibrium as the only historically known practical alternative to order based on empire was not a possible basis for a meaningful contract when equilibrium assumed the rudimentary form of collusion with a third party, China, rather than of a process translating an actually occurring U.S.-Soviet convergence into Russia's informal cooptation.

American policymakers would not consider allowing the Soviets to advance incrementally toward a requisite (i.e., substantial) measure and (substantive, i.e., geopolitical) kind of parity, so as to match tacitly conceded military-technological parity and moderate such parity's extrapolation into policy aims. This refusal deferred contracting for anything more significant than arms control prior to the Soviets' defeat. A post-Soviet Russia was subsequently, although predictably but briefly, willing to enter partnership with America on a junior-status basis and the even more fragile foundation of a disposition to convert gradual convergence into acceptance of the victor's values and institutions virtually overnight. However, a neo-Czarist Russia has no more surprisingly proven unwilling to commit itself to construing cooptation as renunciation of either great-power identity or foreign-policy autonomy.

Rejecting the costs and benefits of both order-upholding empire and status-equalizing equilibrium has meant transferring onto America the triumph-dimming burdens of phantom hegemony, a position replete with paradoxes. A noncoercively implemented preeminence represents an authority that has to be accepted all the more widely because it is solitary and willingly because it lacks enforcement. The full benefits of this awkward situation are contingent on the incumbent possessing most of the tangible and intangible resources required for converting a formal status into effectively performed role. This requisite will overchallenge a polity that, experiencing the potential benefits of a set of technological revolutions, risks being exposed to all the stresses such revolutions imply for societal evolution. As a matter of fact, America's latest leap forward in technological change has already generated more sources of the social distress that calls for reform of either the institutions or the deeper instincts of society than it generates means for attenuating the crisis or mechanisms for realizing the reform.

Moreover, the weight of the paradoxes unavoidably implicit in revolution's encounter with reform on the domestic plane will be augmented by the no less critical interplay between space and time in the international arena. Spatially ordered coexistence of consolidated or emergent strengths with irremediably weak areas or actors whose development has been retarded if not altogether arrested in terms of time reduces, together with the scope of manifest and intrinsically manageable kinds of threat, also occasions for conspicuous external success. Credible foreign policy triumphs are, however, more than useful for a democratic government when a real politically significant socioeconomic or cultural domestic crisis is doubled by a similarly constituted complex of external threats difficult to address on its own: one kind for being diffuse (mass migrations), another for being systemic (economic competitiveness), and still another (from great powers and major civilizations) for being only hypothetical. The speculative character of this most serious longer-term threat extends the time span for identifying the menace precisely and credibly. However, as part of yet another paradox, the technologically accelerated diffusion of communications merely accentuates the decline in the quality of policy thinking by reducing the need for hypothetical reflection and both options-and alternatives-considering anticipation, a debilitating process begun by the telegraph.

A problematically revolutionary and imperatively reform-needy milieu is free of contemporary Americans' disposition to coerce others. It is, however, also sufficiently void of these others' need for America's protection against coercion to minimize spontaneous compliance with America's vision of order. Simultaneously, the substitution of elusive threats to stability for flagrant endangerments of national security translates inevitably, even if only gradually and at first clandestinely, into yet another diminution of American control of events. A milieu replete with elusive dangers to both domestic and global stability makes it probable that the unreliable workings of "interdependence" and potentialities of "integration" will cease to be sufficient. They need to be reinforced with an even but unwritten and primitive global constitution. Conveying its basic principle by more or less explicit terms of a not necessarily signed and sealed contract between the premier world power and unevenly lesser parties is the next item on the global agenda. Tackling the agenda in earnest is possible because its prime contractual instrument is made appropriate by everything—from decreased dependence with respect to well-defined threats to shared helplessness in relation to either undefinable or conventionally unmanageable jeopardy—that currently makes the non-American parties more than usually and more than only nominally equal with the principal party to a new contract.

Discourse I.
About Past and Present:
Salient Challenges and Particular Responses

We approach the third millennium amid an allegedly third, postagricultural and postindustrial, wave in the evolution of society, based on expanding information and expressed in changing quality of knowledge. At the end of an era that did not really start with the end of World War II but rather with the conclusion of larger movements of events, this wave's irrelevance for foreign policy in no way eases the urgency of the search for a new balance in American foreign policy. The most important fifty years of the changes foreign policy is to address began with the earliest onslaught of right-wing totalitarianism on Western civilization in the mid-1930s and have ended with the onset, in the mid-1980s, of the final retreat of Nazism's left-wing Soviet counterpart from its own claim to consummate history by determining its outcome. In a longer perspective, we may trace the beginnings of the forthcoming new era still more significantly to the simultaneous close of one thousand years of the competitive European state system and its initially Eurocentric globalization. Wrapped in this system's dual passing—backward in time to a prestatist pluralism in the West and only potentially eastward in space—is the crisis of a type of realpolitik that was merely simulated in a "cold" war before this "war's" further cooling evolved into the rudiments of a co-imperial peace.

As the two problematically European successors to the western and eastern portions of the Roman Empire weakened internally, Western civilization enjoyed the later stages of its protracted ascent to global preeminence. The mere possibility of its waning reopens the issue of succession, the paramount stake of all politics that culminates when it determines the identity of the regnant civilization. The questions now are, what is to come next and which civilization will then dominate international politics and culture?

When pondering the future of international politics amid manifold uncertainties, it is more appropriate to rely upon prophecy than on prediction. Unlike prediction, which projects trends from past patterns and processes, prophecy must be satisfied with prescription. By melding ominous portents into a brighter promise, prophecy adapts these twin aspects of itself to both material and spiritual concerns of politics. It simultaneously points the way to a tentative return to rather than putative end of history[3] in a world that is turbulently reawakening from a co-imperially managed quasi-peace and awkwardly retracing the formation of Europe. Just as statism recedes in some places, only to be violently reborn in others, similarly scrambled are layers of institutionalized communitarian and primitively chaotic pluralism.

Today's Westerners may well reject the use of force in the forging of states. But this is simply the self-deluding fallacy of a culture that no longer accepts the moral legitimacy of the shedding of blood for any political cause. Moreover, the simultaneous shift from religious fulfillment to material gratification to be found in a larger than tribal community scarcely fills the ensuing spiritual vacuum at the heart of the Occident. Contemporary West is thus at a disadvantage when it reenacts Europe's past encounters with the militancy of Islam and reencounters the challenge of Asia. Dating from the earliest Middle Ages, the cycle of Christian crusades and Muslim countercrusades is replayed in today's aggressive roll-back of yesterday's colonialism. The very fanaticism of this modern countercrusade expresses, however, nothing so much as the continuing decline of the Islamic civilization's inner strength. By contrast, modern China's rising strength offers a more potent challenge to the West, one first encountered when the Enlightenment discovered the Orient and was thus presented with a disturbing cultural alternative to Europe, foreshadowing the ups and downs in China's vitality and, consequently, antagonism toward the West.

Continuities in history will undermine any prophecy that makes a millenarian utopia contingent on the success of a particular technique for improving socioeconomic conditions in a small portion of the world. Conversely, the ongoing return to history builds upon the mere possibility that these conditions might fail to spread sufficiently before they collapse at the center. The prospect of this center's confrontation with other major civilizations contradicts the end-of-history thesis more frontally, but a fatal weakness also besets this ostensibly gloomier vision of the future when it anticipates culture-driven conflict in lieu of consumption-based comity.[4] Consistent with their differently ideological conceptions of world politics, one of the hypotheses plays down continuities in history when it postulates the possibility of its imminent "end"; the other oversimplifies the complexities inherent in the defining attributes of civilization as distinct from culture when it fails to clarify the operationally crucial notion of a "clash." Laxness in defining crucial phenomena obscures the significance for policy of the difference between the societal aspect of civilization, consisting of the rituals of interpersonal conduct, and the technological and institutional attributes related more directly to political power and consequently to the state's (or something like it) relation to society (and its equivalent).

More than the behavioral, the relatively impersonal attributes contrast with the spiritual and artistic responses to the human predicament that define cultures. Whereas their very nature rules out a meaningful ranking or weighing of cultures, the relative standing of major civilizations is directly important for foreign policy. As among the Occidental, the Islamic, and the Oriental civilizations, such standing has varied historically and presently varies unequally with respect to the distinct facets of civilization. It follows that a policy-relevant prophecy must address the narrow political divisions among powers and between elites and masses within particular civilizations as well as civilizations' capacities as powers and their virtues or failings as cultures.

The separate weaknesses of the two prophecies combine to become important in practice when a single phenomenon, relevant for culture as well as civilization and reminiscent of the twilight of another yet vastly more ancient imperial pax, emerges as the principal overt threat to global stability—namely, the mass population migrations across frontiers between states and civilizations. The West's vulnerability to continuing cultural dilution calls for newly effective siegecraft, whereas an imaginative statecraft will be necessary to avoid the West's beleaguerment as a power-wielding and -dependent civilization by other such civilizations. Any workable combination of the ancient science of siegecraft and the classic arts of statecraft, likely to avert a fatal fusion of the two kinds of investment, will require a step back from the mutually reinforcing indulgences of the liberal welfare state and the liberally, if not wastefully, overextended warfare state of the last fifty years. Ironically, the collapse of one, the totalitarian-socialist utopia opened the way for a critical correction of the competing liberal-progressivist utopia at the very moment of its apparent triumph. The insular variety of economically supported military power is similarly subject to revision now that it has celebrated the latest of its late-modern string of victories over its continental rivals' contrary makeup of state power and its relation to society.

The collapse of the assumptions and aspirations that fueled these late indulgences rehabilitates rather than renders obsolete the natural laws of politics of all ages, which compelled and until recently sustained the societal austerities of an earlier age. For the United States, less government at home translates in this context into less appetite for governance globally if the merit of defeating the totalitarian regimes is not to be undone by aimlessly activist diplomacy overreacting to their disappearance. Increasingly, America responds instead by confusing real politics with diplomatic acrobatics; this produces directionless policy at a significant crossroads not only for this country but for world politics itself. Will the primacy of the geopolitical oceanic-insular principle and geopolitical sector, last realized in America's succession to Britain in world leadership, continue? Or will centrality revert to the continental core of the world island, represented today by the German-Russian-Chinese trio? Perceiving the looming crossroads in time and negotiating them with skill would allow America to withdraw, to its advantage, at least part of the way into the safeguarding wings. Ignoring the challenge may well force a retreat at a later stage and annul any benefit that might have accrued from staging the retrenchment in time.

Over the past few decades the United States could plausibly claim the status of a European power, first by helping to save the continent in the Second World War and subsequently by upholding its free half as part of midwifing the beginning of the global extension of the European state system. Yet America's diplomatic posture before and forceful intervention in the first of the German wars had also arguably caused much later damage by deflecting Germany's course from an orderly succession to the waning continental preeminence of France. In the role of insular arbiter, perfected by Britain, America impeded the European system's capacity to renovate itself within and, once reequilibrated around the next premier power, to gradually extend itself without. Conversely, Russia's part in rolling back Germany's reach beyond preeminence to hegemony in the second of the German wars was subsequently invalidated when it enslaved the continent's eastern half. The ability of the Soviets' Czarist precursor to withstand a similar bid by Germany's French predecessor continues nonetheless to earn the right to participate prominently in the concert of great powers for a defeated but liberated Russia within Europe and eventually in the global arena.

The disparate past merits and demerits of America and Russia as controversially European powers are relevant for evaluating and molding their future roles in the face of threats (be they defined in terms of security, stability, or survival) to a West that is both indistinguishably a civilization, caught up in a dialectic among civilizations, and a power exposed to the uncertain prospect of a reactivated balancing among major powers. If it is to retain its position as regnant civilization, and hold off potential claimants to succession, the

West as a whole will have to avoid division and disaggregation as much as it must forestall the unification of the non-Western civilizations qua powers. An appropriate strategy in response to these challenges, one that combines the best of ancient-to-medieval siegecraft, testing endurance, and of more activist statecraft, testing intelligence, will flow from the correct response to a key question: Is it Russia that is individually at a greater and more immediate risk of beleaguerment or is it the West collectively, if only eventually?

Russia's de facto exclusion from greater Europe is apt to foster its progressive disintegration or internal implosion, subsequently usable to vindicate the exclusion. Either outcome will likely produce defensively offensive reactions which, extending from Russia's nearest western neighbors and NATO to its Islamic soft underbelly vis-à-vis China, will ultimately compel a choice for Russia to either compulsively confront the Asian power or compliantly accommodate it. Inasmuch as it is even more certain that Russia's, just as any other state's, confrontation with Islam will encourage forcible Islamic unification under anti-Western extremists, Russia's submissive conciliation with China would tend to unify Asian civilization through a triumphantly ascendant China's magnetic attraction, extending eventually to Japan. The result: Russia's initial, but no less probably the West's ultimate slippage into a state of siege.

In essence, the fundamental question for the West is whether a Eurasian Russia is to become really European or primarily if not wholly Asian. An answer will involve the intertwined components of Russia's historic trinity: autocracy, nationality, orthodoxy. Autocracy cum orthodoxy in Russia translates into a Eurasian personality and policy, as does nationality submerged in orthodoxy. A European alternative requires Russian-style democracy to replace or, more realistically, mitigate autocracy, and a secular nationality to be spiritually sustained by orthodoxy at home but not superseded by politicized religiosity in the shaping of foreign policy regionally. Russia's Europeanization and its democratization are the intertwined facets of a unified process—one that cannot be sliced up in terms of either time or space by trying to orchestrate short-term constraints on Russia with longer-term conciliation of Russia while artificially segregating "little" from "greater" Europe in the process.

A positive resolution of Russia's triadic tension is central to the future unity of Europe and to Russia's positive role within a Euro-Atlantic security structure. If, matching Russia's Europeanization-cum-democratization process, the globalization of China's power and policy is to coincide with the liberalization of Chinese polity, the Middle Kingdom will have to resolve a comparable tension although, conversely from Russia, with a view to exchanging a superiority complex vis-à-vis the West as a civilization for compatibility with the West as equivalent cultures and coexistent powers. It will indicate dominant trends whether China's strategy toward its own "near abroad" collides or meshes consensually with Russia's regional policies. Or is the key to the enigma lodged deeper in the two facets of modernism, and one of traditionalism, which are at play within the Chinese triad?

One modernist facet, a societal pluralism that emphasizes political economy, builds on China's successive post-agricultural and commercial-urban revolutions. It assimilates the long-range development of China as a continental but insulated polity (and in key parts coastal maritime economy) to the kind of evolution experienced by European insular-oceanic polities, creating the basis for similarly evolving foreign policies. The other and immediately more threatening facet of China's modernity is a unitary-centralized statism that has overcome resurfacing disintegrative tendencies. China shares with other continental states the consequences of a close imbrication in a war-prone state system. But, depending on the degree of the country's internal stability and strengths, it also displays a uniquely volatile mixture of opportunistic pragmatism, ideological absolutism, and geostrategic realism. Potentially competing with, or paradoxically condoning, either of the modernist strands, is the traditionalist component associated with the Middle Kingdom. It has repeatedly deflected China's policymakers from realpolitical pragmatism to alternatively isolationist and aggressively expansionist cultural idealism.

Contemporary adaptations of the traditional policies are coupled with the largely ceremonial methods of implementing them. Both will affect the balance between the two distinctive features of Chinese modernism. Thus, all-out power politics would attend the survival of neotraditionalist tendencies into a modern statism, one that emphasizes the military and draws on economic modernization consummated by a centrally controlled blend of societal and administrative pluralism. Before widening into a global policy of retaliation against the onetime colonizing West, this power politics would be felt first regionally from Central Asia to Eastern Siberia and beyond in China's southeast and northeast Asian rimlands and the South China Sea. Alternatively, China could continue moving in the maritime realm and beyond it, in step with the West, toward societal economism and the mercantile objectives of a different brand of modernism.

In essence, one alternative is a Chinese foreign policy that pursues and produces prosperity for individual Chinese with materially consolidating and ideologically disarming effects on Chinese culture. Another is a strategy that aims at generating power for China as a civilization bidding for triumphant if not vengeful succession to the position of global dominance. A China open to the West is encouraged by Sino-American relations that point toward partnership and even co-guarantorship in new security structures. The presumptively adversarial course is implicit in maintaining NATO's present form and denying its anti-Russian thrust. If so, what will discourage modern China from lapsing back into regional hegemonism en route to global revisionism with the backing of its new material strength? Alternatively, who will shield a stressfully modernizing China from collapsing into domestic warlordism with differently destabilizing consequences as a result of economic failure? Since the stark alternatives are clearer than the manner of influencing them from the outside, it will be easier to affect China's grand strategy indirectly than directly.

First, the geostrategic terms: The critical factor is U.S. relations with and attitudes toward Russia, immunizing it against either despondent confrontation or defiant accommodation with China. A revised Euro-Atlantic security architecture with linkages to an East Asian-Pacific counterpart (via Russian membership in both and China's co-guarantor role in the former) is one possible institutional mechanism. Second, in cultural and civilizational terms: Attempts to micromanage China's politico-economic development through intrusive civil rights-centered liberal interventionism will continue to be the least effective policy. To target China's oriental-despotic counterpart to Russia's autocratic tradition is to indulge in a culturally determined approach to trade relations. Such an approach is as futile as was the Middle Kingdom policy of refusing to trade with migrant Mongol barbarians from behind the Wall. Conversely, some influence can accrue from policies based on the awareness that China shares with the West the fundamental problem of defining the cultural scope and contents of any civilization so that it also constitutes a defendable as well as nonthreatening power.

A monocultural little China in the past and multicultural greater China at diverse stages, including the present, have been equally unable to confront the outside world from behind some kind of wall or through a more flexible strategy. In a similar way, a comparatively limited or expanded West is and will continue to be impaled on the horns of this same dilemma. Faced with a quandary, both sides require policies that blend modernism with tradition, injecting a sufficient dose of value-consciousness and historical awareness into ad hoc pragmatism to qualify it as authentically political realism.[5]

Whatever happens in and with China in the long run, the immediate threat to the West is more to its stability than to its traditionally defined security and most of all to its survival as a vital civilization. A state of siege that originates in a phenomenon (population migrations) may be easily linked up with a process (involving major powers and civilizations). The effort to avoid either or both commands a defense strategy that is very different from one bequeathed by the terminated instalment of the protracted East-West conflict. Refighting a quasi-war diplomatically with respect to an obsolete military alliance is no better than refighting a real one militarily on the battlefield. An attempt to do so risks producing a Russian version of interwar Weimar and will nullify, by the mere fact of ignoring, the intervening positive changes in the *Zeitgeist* that underscore differences in the spirit of today's Russia compared to yesterday's Germany.

Instead of arming a static perimeter with a marginally enlarged North Atlantic Alliance that antagonizes Russia, a more elastic and dynamic approach to the defense of the West will successively accommodate political, economic, and military degrees or stages of threat in association with Russia. Elastic defense becomes automatically one in depth because it is aimed at blunting or absorbing penetrations at both the territorial margins (Russia) and the operational margins (cultural and geopolitical before economic and military) while immediately preserving and ultimately depending on capabilities held in reserve in the strategic rear. Repositioning the American core of such a reserve from the frontline to a last-resort defender preserves a crucial capability held in trust for the West in ultimate emergencies rather than weakens an eminently replaceable defense structure represented by NATO in its present form. For its part, a United States freed of inessential encumbrances can interpose itself impartially between the reactionary-to-moderately conservative and the moderately reformist-to-radical elements in Islam. It can do the same between a China that has not been antagonized by a United States that reacted on behalf of Russia too late to be circumspect about it, and a Japan that had not been irreversibly attracted to an apparently all-powerful China, or alienated from a United States overinvolved in Europe.

Instead of validating the clash of civilizations by congealing them into hostile power blocs, an elastic approach preserves or even expands the opportunities for multiple interest-based alignments across divides between civilizations, nation-states, and social classes. Such tactically inspired collusions have in post-Cold War conditions already shaped the Gulf War, just as they had centuries earlier consistently muted the controversy between Islam and Christendom. An effective security structure for the future is, therefore, one that has discarded the simplicities of the immediate past—the U.S.-Soviet-Chinese triangle and the two-camps alliance system—for contemporary ambiguities in international relations and will reflect the unwieldiness of relations in its own complexity. Although there is presently only a remote threat of the need for the use of force among major states, even an unlikely contingency has to be integrated into present diplomacy and an evolving security architecture perpetuate immemorial precedent as a matter of expediency or prudence. Nevertheless, the overall grand strategy of the West must also respect a measure of change that verges on reversal in the determinative primacy of stakes and procedural priority of mechanisms that favors political stability over military security.

One kind of strategy, which has inertially continued from its abundant late practice, aims at several essentially static outcomes—ranging from stalemate to the dominance of one side—within the traditional balance-of-power dynamic. A more appropriate kind of strategy, which has now reemerged from its late dormancy, pursues stability through an equilibrium more complex than one dependent on ponderous counterweights—wherein, therefore, institutions and instruments of military security are but one and not the most important factor and agency. This more dynamic approach merely formalizes a spontaneous redistribution of assets and liabilities institutionally, without attempting to freeze any of the stages of an ongoing evolution in place. Alert statecraft monitors the process but abstains from efforts to micromanage developments through rigid, let alone antagonistic, organizations. In such conditions, a flexible structure can best be fostered by inaction of some states that induces others to act in their place and in a common interest. Implementation of this strategy rules out, among other things, offers of organizational solutions such as those within NATO or WEU that divert the countries between Germany and Russia from cooperative, including confederative, arrangements that would stabilize the region in depth and for the long run. That such presumptive solutions of an overadvertised problem of security are for domestic reasons immediately more attractive to local regimes than widely unpopular and immediately unrewarding attempts to resolve intra-regional differences locally does not make them better suited to integrate the eastern half of Europe step by necessary step into one genuinely unified Europe.

A suitable recipe for dealing with a not altogether new situation is one that renounces the temptation to erect a new (if initially invisible) Maginot Line beyond the Vistula in favor of the interwar Locarno concept, which reconstructed the division between France and Germany into a potential for cooperation by treating both countries equally as potential aggressors. Applying the formula to Eastern Europe can mean only one thing: safeguarding Western Europe against attack from Russia, and Russia from assault originating in Western Europe. One possible method to implement this reciprocal assurance would be the commitment of both sides not to enter the Visegrad countries from the west and Ukraine and the Baltic states from the east or south militarily by either aggression or alliance. As a first step, these complementary engagements could be provisionally integrated within an overarching security structure such as the Organization for Security and Cooperation in Europe (OSCE). Furthermore, they could and, indeed, would have to be guaranteed by the United States (replacing Britain and Italy in the interwar Locarno original's Rhine Pact). The countries between Germany and Russia would be neither demilitarized nor neutralized but could, instead, impartially implement their natural politico-diplomatic role as an active link between the two regional great powers. By automatically enlarging the West, the Locarno formula would resurrect the historic function of eastern Europe as the bulwark vis-à-vis pressures from still farther east. However, whereas Europe's east acts now under this hypothesis in association with the core West, rather than isolated from it, the West as a whole takes care to avoid prematurely and unnecessarily provoking either China or Islam.

While superficially similar, the Locarno formula therefore differs materially from a non-aggression pact between a North Atlantic Alliance expanded eastward and either Russia or the Commonwealth of Independent States. Under the cover of formal equality, that arrangement would effectively signify the Russia-centered side's material inferiority while implicitly assigning it a more than even share of aggressiveness. Moreover, and not less prejudicially, it would symbolically recall the ominously ambiguous circumstances and motivations surrounding the non-aggression formula when it was being promoted by the totalitarian regimes along the road to World War II.

In lieu of expanding the North Atlantic Alliance conservatively but nonetheless too widely in its present form and functions, a radical solution would limit the coalition's successor in functions while expanding its membership drastically. A new Euro-Atlantic Treaty Organization, which confines itself to perpetuating the disbanded alliance's military culture, skeletal command-and-control structure, and research-and-development agenda, can include Russia without providing China, the only imaginable military threat and as such legitimate alliance target other than Russia, with a valid pretext for antagonistic reactions. Such a Euro-Atlantic structure could further avoid antagonism if it was coordinated with a comparably self-limiting Asian-Pacific security system, as part of which China could eventually join the United States as a co-guarantor in Europe and its Islamic borderlands, while Japan would do the same as between Russia and China in Asia. The resultant depolarization of the global security structure would reflect China's obvious stake in opposing an overpowering consolidation of the western half of Eurasia from either direction and Japan's identical concern over the eastern half of the megacontinent.

It is true that under a co-guarantee the guarantors are expected to act in concert and refrain from arbitrary unilateral actions in the arena where motivation might be suspect. However, this proviso neither need block action by either of the guarantors, including the United States, within the framework of either the Asian-Pacific or the Euro-Atlantic association nor must it do so. To ensure this, the two parallel and complementary regional security systems would have to be conceived and constructed so as to be able to reconcile two key functions. One of them concerns intraregional disturbances of a low order of intensity and equally limited interregional security issues, and would be addressed by the several guarantors in concert. The other function concerns nuclear challenges, either overt major power threats affecting the critical strategic boundaries or a covert lesser state blackmail implicit in ongoing nuclear proliferation. The guarantors would have to remain free to react to these contingencies one way or another in the last resort and at their individual risk.

A dynamically evolving security architecture of this kind would enable the United States to partially disengage from its now-customary European presence in order to pursue an intercivilizational strategy in Asia, while acting in relation to powers inside and outside the West as a truly effective buffer or partner, balancer or guarantor—anything but an ineffectual meddler. To be sure, any substantial reduction in U.S. responsibilities in Europe would entail a hypothetical future cost to the continent's defense. Offsetting this deficit entails upgrading the role of Germany and Russia, the two victims of revolution and vehicles of totalitarianism spawned by a war diverted from timely pacification by the prospect of American intervention. A partnership between Russia and Germany is better for Europe and for the West than either party's separate special relationship with America, which would only discriminate against the other European powers. Renewed entente with Germany will reposition Russia firmly within a European and, by extension, global concert of powers (or, eventually, regions or civilizations). It would also block either partner from a preeminence that might escalate to hegemony in all of Europe pursuant to competition over dominance in Eastern Europe. The danger of such a competition, invoked as the grounds for NATO's rapid but restricted expansion eastward, is not negligible despite its uncertain practical meaning in contemporary conditions. The stakes are still higher, however, because the structures to be shaped by grand strategy reach deeper and wider. Relations among civilizations highlight the importance of the geographic scope and aggregate power potential of a variously delimitable West, a quantitative dimension that is only analytically distinct from the kind of Russia and by extension Europe variable strategies can be expected to foster within a West beleaguered on the South-North plane actually and the East-West axis potentially.

En route to fashioning degrees of Russian participation, contemporary Europe can condone an imperial but essentially democratic Russia as an active participant in its affairs and Western civilization. Or it must endure a purely national but near inevitably autocratic Russia as a passively truculent buffer between rival civilizations encroaching on a reconstituted Muscovy from several sides. Reducing a Russia-centered imperial federation to ethnically homogenous Russian polity would not create anything like a quantitatively equal counterpart to an expanded NATO that excluded it. Nor would a strictly national Russia be any more likely to become democratic than to cease being imperialistic because it could not, consistently with its narrowed identity, abandon ethnic Russians or Russian-speakers in the "near abroad." Only an imperial Russian Federation can, and under favorable conditions will, be willing to exchange a tolerant attitude toward the nationality policies of the states on its border for their Russia-friendly foreign policies. Conversely, a truncated Russia, reduced to the condition of a passive buffer between Europe and Asia, would constitute a standing invitation to either China or, down the road, Germany to court it and, having become the omnipotent arbiter between Russia and Europe, assume diplomatic dictatorship over what was left of Europe.

By the same token, only an America relieved of obsolete domestic and foreign burdens will become a more effective balancer inside Eurasia and greater Asia than it can hope to be in Europe alone as an intrusive and closely entangled meddler. Moreover, this country would be also freer to shape the worldwide South-North issue of unwanted population migrations that shift the strategic perspective past the "third Rome" and its relation to the West to that of the West toward the "Fourth" World. On both accounts the historicist perspective on strategy gravitates usefully not only from medieval to modern Islam and from an early to late modern Middle Kingdom to contemporary China, but past both to an initially conquering but eventually fatally beleaguered civilization of antiquity—the first Rome.

A part-latent and part-acute crisis reflects the present transition from two near-equal poles of concentrated military-political power to two segments of unevenly crystallized power, articulated processes, and diffuse phenomena. The latently conventional segment of comparatively well-defined powers continues to be centered on the balance of power as its operational norm in the last resort. Its main strategic theater, the German-Russian-Chinese Eurasian triangle, is affected by the United States as the more western of the insular wing powers and last-resort balancers and impacts Japan as the eastern one. The attendant crisis potential is dormant, inherently manageable, but subject to globally disruptive ramifications if it is not addressed by appropriate strategies. The other segment exhibits a state-of-nature type of politics among pre- and substate actors. Localized upheavals revolve around ethno-cultural differences that do not necessarily impart to the turbulence an ethically legitimizing rationale, but equip it with a politically critical mass expressed in either parochial civil wars or a virtual worldwide class war. This kind of crisis is not manageable either locally or at a distance. It also lacks an inherent potential for spreading significantly so long as the local disturbances do not infiltrate the major-power segment or impinge upon it by escalating the ongoing population migrations.

When concern gravitates coincidentally from process to phenomenon—from interactions among more or less organized units of power to massive movements of populations—the focus shifts from statecraft to siegecraft. Interplay between process and phenomenon is bound to intensify the interpenetration of civilization with culture, just as a transition from stylized statism to disorderly pluralism complicates the shift between the two basic approaches to defense and offense. Siegecraft tests the comparative material and moral endurance between besieger and besieged, whereas skills predominate in flexible maneuver on the diplomatic chessboard of statecraft as much as on the open field of battle in warfare. The West's siege by escapees from the Fourth World does not call for building a Great Wall any more than erecting another Maginot Line would profit statecraft. The encounters of civilization with barbarians in ancient China and with outright barbarism in modern Europe are too different from today's challenges to recommend exactly reproductive responses. The question of the day is therefore whether the strategies that evolved during the Cold War can be adapted to the newly insurgent Fourth World periphery on the South-North axis better or less well than to the Eurasian great-power core along the West-East axis.

What, if any, is the link between the core (West-East) and the contextual (North-South) issues and between statecraft and siegecraft? What kind of Russian rapport with the West or Western policy toward Russia will alleviate or aggravate the dirty secret behind much of U.S. and European foreign policies? No kind of Russia, whether internally united or disintegrating, European or Eurasian, can materially assist either the beleaguered North or the besieging South in the foreseeable future. On the South-North issue's specifically Islamic front, however, a favorably evolving Russia might be able to assist Europe culturally by drawing upon its experience as a multicultural polity and its privileged relations with some Islamic countries or regimes in foreign policy. Conversely, and more certainly, a chaotic Russia that has set off a massive wave of escapees would seriously aggravate migrations from east to west. Thus, at least in this respect, a Western statecraft that is farsighted on the geostrategic Eurasian issue with civilizational connotations will positively affect the prospects for an effective as well as enlightened defensive siegecraft on the ostensibly politico-economic but ultimately culture-centered plane of special concern to the core-Western societies. Absent conditions that realize a hypothetical end of history, the result is a paradox: Central to coping with the most acute issue of the day, resistant to the most sophisticated techniques of siegecraft, is statecraft over the provisionally muted traditional stakes among major powers and allegedly clashing civilizations. Moreover, it is the very latency of these classic stakes that challenges strategic imagination most and raises questions about the nature of world politics that are more tantalizing for theory and more frustrating for policy than has been the case for decades if not centuries in more clearly defined conditions.

Interrogation I.
A Civil War:
Symptom or Emblem?

At the close of the twentieth century, the turmoil in Bosnia-Herzegovina amounted to an *abscès de fixation* on the global body politic: a particularly inflamed boil concentrating distempers released from the regionally constraining effects of global conflict. Bereft of strategic guideposts, ineffectual diplomacy proved unfit to lance the boil with calming effects on the larger organism. Yet if Bosnia was in part symptom and in part self-contained pathology, a correspondingly two-sided question arises: what insights into the nature of the global environment could have been derived from a timely sympathetic understanding of the symptom, and what larger conclusions and consequences follow from America's actual response to the regional crisis if the response is emblematic of this country's evolving fundamental posture?

What have been the constituents of the Bosnian, far from unique, problem with respect to the principal actors? Among the local actors, the Serbian party exhibited a tribal-agrarian atavism fixated on land and, secondarily, religion in an essentially medieval cast, which stood diametrically opposed to the secularized urban-commercial multiculturalism of the comparatively modern mindset and values of the Muslims. This basic dichotomy was in itself sufficient to inflame the core of the civil-cum-confessional conflict, waged directly over fixed and finite land and only indirectly and prospectively over strategically significant territory. The postures of the European major powers, specifically Germany, France, and Russia, illustrated the prevalent mix of traditional statist—strategic or only formally diplomatic—stakes, and trade-centered economic interests: the former expressed in the attenuated historic attachments and diluted geopolitical stakes aligning Germany on the side of Croatia and, in different degrees, France and Russia on that of Serbia;

the latter illustrated in the fading or currently undefinable link between geostrategic role, guaranteeing continuing presence, and material resource, expressed in the present costs and hypothetical future profits of a successful engagement ensuring future access.

Finally, even more confusing are the disparate considerations obtaining in the United States: one anchored in the symbolism of leadership to be demonstrated as a matter of popular expectation and presidential obligation; the other rooted in the equally compelling imperative to avoid the tangible costs in blood or treasure of a significant and, therefore, risk-fraught involvement. A moralism innate to political culture, unable to come to terms with the disparity between the values and expressions of Bosnian medievalism and American progressivism, consummated the confusion. Introducing apparent clarity into actual incompatibilities necessitated a neat distribution of condemnation, targeted at the presumptive aggressor, and indignation, on behalf of its declared victims. Inevitably sacrificed was the combination of effective action with provisional abstention from final ethical judgment until after wartime propaganda has been censored by reestablished peace in the interest of truth.

At the diplomatic and strategic core of such contradictions was a conflict implanted in the Euro-American relationship. Treating ex-Yugoslavia generally and Bosnia in particular as European issues encouraged a nominal delegation of responsibility to the Europeans. In fact, however, the American leadership requisite ruled out a strictly European solution as a matter of both procedure—a devolutionary mandate Europe could not lastingly evade—and product, an arbitrated or enforced settlement the local parties could not indefinitely withstand. Subtly intertwined with the constituents of the resulting policy quandaries were dilemmas and attendant distortions of both a normative and an existential kind. One set of dilemmas centered on contrasting values, another was revealed in the neglected difference between substance and procedure.

What was the comparative substantive justice or merit of the conflicting claims of the parties? The case for the (Bosnian) Serbs could be plausibly founded in both an ethical and a real political implausibility. Imitating other and better qualified fragments of Yugoslavia, official Bosnia would unilaterally defect from a common state sustained in two world wars by the Serbs' peculiar, and on the face of it now obsolete, warrior mentality with great strategic advantage for some of their principal present critics. Could these defections be peacefully combined with that once-dominant majority's reduction to an at-best subordinate minority status in the successor states, historically nonexistent (Bosnia-Herzegovina) or hostile (Croatia)? The answer is supplied by the history of all major (including Western) states, which enshrines the immutable principles and immemorial custom constitutive of Europe—a different matter from present predispositions and feelings. Whereas the Serbs appealed to the brutal facts that make up an integral part of historic continuity, the Muslims invoked the values of multicultural community implicitly inimical to the Serbs' tribal and rural identity. While eroding this identity, the pretense of cultural neutrality would automatically promote the urban-commercial assets and propensities of the Muslims with subtly more threatening long-term effects on the position of the Serbian minority than any plausible local expression of Islamic fundamentalism. Implicit in multiculturalism—as opposed to historic statism—is universal consent and equal practical advantage of all participant parties. The entire history of the area, except when subject to alien control or extraneous coordination, argues against its practicality as an option—least of all one promulgated unilaterally.

With the opening of hostilities, disinterest in or lack of agreement on the substantive pluses and minuses moved the focus of attention inexorably to procedure. In procedural terms, likewise well-documented historically, the supposedly necessary or at least commonly asserted connection is between the initiator of hostilities and the perpetration of atrocities—a linkage illustrated in the Bosnian case on the sequence from (Serbian) aggression to ethnic cleansing and their compression into war crimes. The lopsided distribution or attribution of culpabilities was, other things being equal, implicit in the redistribution of emphasis from substantive merit (or justification) to procedural method (or execution). This once again not unusual wartime subtext of blame-assigning could be saved from ethical and political pitfalls only by interlocking substance creatively with procedure in the making of peace.

Prior to the conflict's eruption, basically positive (because in some way activist) approaches by the major powers could have been either preemptive or negative. A substantively preemptive approach entailed an extraneously imposed redistribution and relocation of the ethnically heterogeneous populations along lines, ensuring a minimum of homogeneity, and economic viability for all or at least the principal constituents of former Yugoslavia. In terms of international law, the procedurally negative approach required the nonrecognition of the secessionist entities until their self-declared governments have demonstrated a de facto capacity and a dependable willingness: ability to effectively control the claimed territory and disposition to take steps sufficient in objective judgment to progressively convert the minority's initial tolerance of the new situation into identification with a consolidated order. Absent such evidence, the political corollary to the denial of legal recognition is avoidance of extraneous intervention. Abstention would then allow the dynamic of violent local restabilization to run its course in clarifying the actual relationship of forces as a basis for lasting stability to be codified in an eventual settlement.

Toleration of local escalation, implicit in the negative strategy, was consistent with measures for the prevention of the conflict's expansion. But neither the approach nor the desideratum was consistent with the greater powers projecting a mismatch between the role they claimed and the resource they were prepared to deploy into a confused and confusing melange of actual interference and formal nonintervention—a confusion doomed to grow with the admixture of increasingly fearful concern about the involvement of a third (non-Western Islamic) party to deepening moral condemnation of only one of the directly engaged parties. Abstention from preemptive surgery at the beginning of the civil war had signaled indifference to substance. The actually adopted expedients for pacifying the conflict in its second halftime reflected the growing fixation on procedure. This trend allowed the successive peace formulas to consistently lag behind military facts on the ground, for fear of "rewarding aggression." The result was combining well-intentioned (UN-run) humanitarian palliatives, as substitutes for the previously shunned surgery, with dubiously conceived (EU-centered) diplomatic initiatives in lieu of effective interposition. Charitable UN engagement was difficult to reconcile in principle with NATO's armed intervention; an attempt to coordinate the two contrary courses was incompatible with the (U.S. Congress') priority to arm the Muslims. Coordination yielded to connivance when the parallel approaches were mainly purchasing a deferral for U.S. military engagement on the ground (improvidently pledged to shield the UN's withdrawal) at the cost of continuing exposure of French, English, and associated UN peacekeepers to retaliation by the Serbs (in case of air strikes) or by either local party (in case of withdrawal).

In light of differently mismanaged initial and midterm approaches, a more successful end-game pointed to a militarily (and economically) underwritten imposition of peace by the greater powers under the cover of negotiations with and among the belligerents. To be both equitable and effective, such an imposition had to reflect a range of facts and satisfy a number of requisites if substantively fair terms were to emanate from a formally correct procedure.

The facts concern, in increasing practical importance, the distribution of substantive rights and wrongs, merits and demerits; the military situation on the ground; and, last but not least, the belligerents' comparative capacity as distinct from their presumptive disposition to challenge the settlement. The last point was crucial because it affected not only the probability of having to enforce the terms, but also the prospects for forceful revanchism eroding regional stability in the longer run. Moreover, in a system of interconnected parts, the procedure of arriving at substantive terms of pacification will necessarily involve inter- and intragreat-power factors. In the Bosnian case this has meant relations among the great European powers and between them and the United States; among domestic political players inside the United States; and between the West and Islam on the plane of civilizations. Institutionalizing these interrelations was predictably a matter of alternative venues for the peace settlement, ranging from (1) a peace conference under Euro-American auspices through (2) a European mandate to the United States as the executor of a Western consensus to (3) America's abstention from direct involvement in favor of a carte blanche to Europe.

The first two formulas have in the Bosnian case principally concerned—and would in comparable future circumstances—the Euro-American relationship. The second and third formulas bear equally or more on domestic American politics. Important in either case for the United States specifically, and the Western powers more generally, is the difference between a decisive intervention at an appropriate time and intermittently continuous while persistently ineffectual meddling; in brief, the difference between grand strategy and gratuitously intrusive diplomacy.

In regard to domestic American politics, expressing presidential leadership through a substantive peace initiative under the first two formulas employs the third formula, however implicitly, as the credibly threatened unacceptable alternative. Employing this leverage effectively will automatically strengthen the executive branch against the legislative in the making of foreign policy and at the end of the day consolidate the president's standing with the third party to the domestic American political triangle, the public. Immediately more important is whether the particulars of the initiative are of a kind to reactivate public support for incurring the moral-political costs of leadership—inherent in any realistic peace terms—and the material costs, implicit in the possibility (declining with the terms' realism) of having to enforce the terms militarily and the (concurrently rising) probability of having to reinforce them economically. If this does not happen, the initiative as well as the response to it, just as before its absence, will only reveal the present vacuity of the leadership myth with only potentially beneficial consequences over an incalculable period of time.

Making the proposed settlement realistic in terms of factual criteria entailed terms basically favorable for the Serbian side even after its battlefield setbacks at the hands of the Croatian-Muslim confederation-cum-military coalition. This necessity collided with congressional and popular opposition to rewarding the Serbs for their misdemeanors. Yet ultimately decisive will be the inverse relationship between the public's (and therefore the congressional majority's) support for the terms and the probability of having to enforce them militarily. The smaller the probability, the greater the support for the settlement would be at the end of the day.

As distinct from the domestic, the globally operative triangle involves the United States with the (West) Europeans and both with international Islam. In this setting, U.S. noninvolvement (the third of the abovementioned peacemaking formulas) is operationally most significant by being presently only hypothetical. A credible decision to abstain, demonstrating America's principled readiness for a strategy of devolution, would automatically disclose divisions on substantive peace terms among the Europeans. Absent U.S. diplomatic engagement, these divisions would easily slide into the traditional pattern of a Franco-Russian entente against Germany, with Britain trying to act as the mediating balancer-arbiter. The Europeans have consequently been faced with the choice between reactivating tolerance for U.S. involvement and stepping up the coordination of national foreign policies on a particularly unpromising issue under stress—a not too difficult quandary easily resolved for the time being by weighing differences with the United States against differences among themselves and measuring the tactical advantages of a party that stays out of a tangled situation while keeping its options open against the strategic costs and questionable benefits of irreversibly militant engagement.

Even an only hypothetical scenario along these lines does some good, however. It discloses practical longer-term benefits from clarifying latent or dormant ambiguities and animosities on a substantively secondary but symbolically salient issue, capable of injecting greater seriousness into Maastricht-type pledges of foreign policy coordination. Immediately more to the point was the certainty of American participation in active peace making, once it had been set off by whatsoever and initiated by whosoever, lest consistent U.S. abstention finally compel Europe's self-differentiation in the foreign policy field. American concern to forestall a "premature" development of this kind enables an internally coordination-ready Europe to match the U.S. leverage implicit in the hypothesis of America's self-removal from the diplomatic scene. In the absence of all-European coordination, only token rewards for separate U.S.-friendly initiatives—such as France's Chirac's—will be forthcoming.

The conjunction of concerns of this kind with late-stage military stalemate was in the event necessary, but also sufficient, to propel U.S. diplomacy into an active effort to formalize the spontaneously emerging terms of a both realistic and equitable settlement. Intersection of substantive interests and positions with partly conventional and partly improvised procedural mechanisms produced a fair test for the ability of American sympathy for the Muslims to countervail an overtly Russian (and covertly Anglo-French?) pro-

Serb bias, while American engagement alone could mediate between this particular sympathy and the Germans' pro-Croatian commitment. Finally, and not least importantly, a U.S.-wrought corrective to any latent anti-Muslim biases of Europeans exposed more directly to the Islamic threat was sufficient to appease Islam's increasingly alienated moderates until hoped-for economic growth on all sides will have absorbed the contending atavisms. Under such circumstances, purging contrary predispositions through formally consensual diplomatic interactions is apt to bring into the open conditions and terms of settlement implicit in the "facts," without doing violence to respective merits and felt rights of the local contestants.

Playing out such a scenario on a specific and timely issue creates a basis for more fundamental readjustments in Euro-American relations by revealing the conditions of cooperation productive for both sides and the costs as well as potential benefits of its alternatives. By the same token, merely to consider the prerequisites and precepts governing a particular peace settlement suggests its generic conditions. Absent a materially underwritten preemption of military contention, these conditions comprise three successive stages.

The first stage of deliberate abstention has been identified under the rubrics of initial nonrecognition of a peaceably unsustainable revision of the status quo and subsequent noninterference with the violent local workings of political nature in and for restabilization. Notably when this negative posture has been shunned or its potential mismanaged, the second stage will consist of midterm demonstration of costly contradictions inherent in attempts to substitute diplomatic and other half-measures for calculated massive intervention at a time and in the place of the outsider's or outsiders' choosing. The third and final stage can and ought to be that of a determined and appropriately dramatic injection of the major powers into a situation sufficiently matured in terms of the local parties' demonstrated capabilities and prospective risks and benefits from accepting or rejecting an interposition aimed at an equitable conflict resolution.

For the institutional and procedural resources of the major powers to be injected into staging a peace process effectively, an initiative sustained by a vision of the outcome and consistent with its initiators' and executors' respective interests and capabilities will have to reflect the local subjects' substantive merits and potentials rather than procedural demerits and propensities. Moreover, economic resources of the major powers for reinforcing the settlement and the political will to enforce it if challenged must be available for sustaining the process and consolidating its product when it has materialized. The outsiders will find the economic investment and military commitment to be more domestically acceptable if the investment reduces the probability of having to honor even a correspondingly reduced commitment in full. Economic assistance is more likely to help stabilize a region in the aftermath of a military encounter among the prospective recipients than prior to and in lieu of the violent catharsis.

Not only will subsequent immersion in material reconstruction usefully complement exhaustion from war in consolidating the appeasement, but pacification will permit a fairer appreciation of the ethical issues raised by the conflict than was possible during its course. Ideally, the factual (even if only partial) victors, imbued with the sense of substantive rightness of their cause, might then be anxious to cleanse the method of defending this cause from hurtful imputations, provided a politic reexamination of all aspects of the case rather than formally juridical adjudication of individual deeds taken out of the violent context improved on the practice of victors judging the defeated. Finally, how the Bosnian boil has been lanced will disclose much about the relationship between predicament and promise and between high foreign and low domestic politics in the West. Since Bosnia was symptomatic of the impact of ethnic and creedal enmities on peace and stability, excising surgically the abscess that concentrated the wider malaise might have restored a measure of health to a body politic larger than the former Yugoslavia. Doing so was beyond the will and capacity of a Western Europe where real politics has acquired the status of last-resort reserve and residual mind-set, surviving mainly to interfere with the routines of municipal-type communitarian politics sufficiently entrenched to defeat resolutions to resuscitate a collective Raison d'État. All the more important for Europe's eastern half become the questions why and how America finally responded to the crisis. The resumption of American peace-making diplomacy at the head of newly cooperative West Europeans in the late summer of 1995 offered one more chance to undo earlier hesitancies and refurbish a tarnished image. Was the impression justified and is the implied promise reliable?

American diplomatic leadership was resumed in response to a set of coincidences: Croatian military success in the Serb-occupied part of Croatia and Serb-threatened section of Bosnia, a new and for his own reasons newly cooperative French president, and Bosnian Serb military-strategic and propaganda miscalculations—all of these coincidences being more important than America's "Machiavellian" collusion with the Croats. The luster of the last-mentioned tactical plus is dimmed by leaving intact the strategic premise and precondition of resolute American action: The United States could and would lead only when others did the fighting (the Croats) or the dying (including the French and other UN peacekeepers) and would itself fight only in cases of actually or at least plausibly compelling economic significance (e.g., the Gulf War), provided others bore much or most of the financial cost and most or all of the fighting could take place from the relative safety of the air. Erecting a "phantom" hegemony on so fragile a basis means that, not unusually for this kind of role and status, sustaining preeminence will wholly depend on the revocable connivance of still weaker and less resolute friendly or unfriendly others.

So long as the favorable prerequisites obtained with respect to Bosnia, medium-term costs to local and regional stability could and would be ignored. Consolidating a revisionist Slav-orthodox anti-Western alliance in the Balkan "powder keg" and mystifying most of the other east-central and eastern Europeans as regards the staying power of America's regional engagement are among the deferred diffuse costs, provisionally concentrated in the future of NATO as a military agent in the short run and diplomatic-political factor more lastingly. Russia's exclusion (over its protests) from the violent last-minute part of the "peace process" could not but deepen its opposition to the newly bellicose coalition's extension into areas of geopolitical or historic Russian interests. Moreover, whereas the alliance's display of military muscle and political resolve automatically encouraged aspirants to membership to press their candidacy, they were even more likely than before to be disappointed when an aggrieved Russia had been mollified by the concession of additional and possibly terminal delays.

In the still longer term, and most ominously, NATO's centrality projects present conditions into a parallel with the interwar period at its most pathological. The task of filling the gap between the responsibilities of victory and the will as well as capacity of the European democracies to meet them was then assigned to two ostensibly contrary devices: one, institutionalized legality posing as morality (in the form of the League of Nations even more than, but essentially not unlike, the United Nations today); the other, a nakedly military instrument. Winston Churchill's exclamation "Thank God for the French Army!" uttered in the earlier setting echoes today in the unstated benediction of the U.S. air force, acting de facto outside or formally within the alliance. In actual fact, more than one unrealistic expectation and hazardous policy had been predicated on the French army's performance only to be dashed in short order. So also the U.S. air force has already demonstrated its inability to make up for all the rest—in Vietnam, without the consequent loss of America's regional credibility engendering all or most of the locally feared consequences for unforeseeable fortuitous reasons; in the Persian Gulf, when ground action, albeit powerfully facilitated from the air, was in the end necessary and its political consequences remained uncertain; and, in the last resort, in Bosnia insofar as NATO's more clinical than therapeutic application of "deliberate force" coincided with and merely consolidated a basic inter-Serbian decision to exchange a diminishing war-making capability on one (Bosnian) side and growing sanctions-induced economic distress on the other (Belgrade) side for an acceptable peace.

Looming behind weaknesses in the field of peace-making diplomacy and warfare alike is America's special problem with tragedy and political passion. At the bottom of a misapprehended relationship between politics and ethics is the seeming inability to apprehend the passions aroused by a contention between contrary rights felt equally strongly and upheld equally ruthlessly by parties to what only on this condition becomes an authentic tragedy, manifested by stoically endured cost in human suffering. The result is reluctance to live with moral ambiguity and the preference for a manichean perspective on the world, always on the lookout for an evil contestant to criminalize and a virtuous one that is being victimized to exonerate. Blindness to the moral complexities and hazards of classic tragedy transforms the American into a congenital outsider vis-à-vis much that is afoot in the world at large; the failure to grasp and (therefore) the inability to live up to tragedy's other side—the tragic heroism that ethically cleanses and may uplift the hegemonic ambition—disqualifies America as a leader so long as it is unwilling to incur the costs and pay the price of a de facto hegemonical position and rarely admitted aspiration. The two handicaps merge when the inability to empathize with the passions of others translates into one's own diminished ability to experience passion in behalf of any cause that does not enable the "average" American to view himself/herself as the victim of society's (past) injustice.

Contemporary America's mass culture is dedicated to material self-indulgence and political apathy most of the time. Fascination with technologies of all kinds (including military) expresses a more deeply inborn penchant for the concrete and tangible over the elusive and complex. If unchanged, this mind-set is questionably equipped to uphold leadership within a global environment divided materially, but not tangibly, and politically, but mainly psychologically, between the haves and the have-nots—and split morally between self-perceived victims and indicted victimizers. In such an environment, a military proficiency that makes it possible, and a military instrumentality that makes it easy, to chastise a designated disturber of peace or order with virtual impunity is questionably emblematic of a positive capacity for leadership.

Discourse II.
About the Two Cities of Man:
Insecure Prosperity and Rebelling Poverty

Political culture and political economy are closely intertwined in the tie between technological revolution and social change. The two are nowhere more intimately imbricated internationally than along the South-North divide standing for the cleavage between the global haves and the have-nots, the socioeconomic significance of which is matched, and in the long run may be overshadowed, by cultural implications that exceed those latent in the Eurasian segment.

Unlike a prediction based on projection from past structures and processes, a prophecy rules out prediction in favor of prescription. If the prescription is to conform with prophecy's dual thrust, it must incorporate ominous portents so as to set off a distant promise. It reflects, then, the tension inherent in the likewise dual nature of politics, involving thrust for power and restraining norm; of man, possessed of physical and metaphysical needs; and of polity, that compounds societal with statist features or is cleft between them. All of these givens are in one way or another more vital than the ephemeral social systems and more compelling than the cerebral ideologies or constitutional mystiques that were lately invoked to obscure the identity of the latest and possibly last geostrategic contention between a continental and an insular-oceanic power extending worldwide from its center in Europe. However, if the present portents are to be exorcized and the chance for any prescription to realize its promise is to be preserved for a particular civilization, without being reserved for it alone, this prescription must express civilization's intimate connection with a particular culture. Doing so requires the will to safeguard a sense of internally coherent identity, capable of mustering the ideal as well as the material resources for self-affirmation. Moreover, definable identity of Western civilization and culture cannot be usefully considered in terms of a problematic member such as Russia alone, any more than conservatism can be defined only in terms of the market, law and order, and military defenses.

It is in this perspective that a phenomenon, mass population migrations across frontiers between states and civilizations, has been emerging as the key immediate threat to global stability and the West's cultural identity. These population movements are the dramatic focus of post-Cold War world politics from the Caribbean via the Mediterranean to the plains of Eastern Europe, and widespread concern about them actually underlies more readily avowable reasons for many a foreign policy. Meanwhile, the problems related to this phenomenon engage in an intricately seamless web all the particular issues that outlived the late conflict and ascend anew to prominence as a result of its demise: the relationship between domestic and foreign politics, between economics and security policies, and between civilian and military cultures and establishments—all converging and colliding in ethno-religious and sociopolitical conflicts caught up in biologically shaped demographics and propagated by the awesome marvels of telecommunications technology. Addressing the serious pragmatic and ethical complications introduced thus into the enduring conflict between the political necessities of self-help and self-defense and the moral imperatives of compassion and community responsibly eludes more than many the facile recipe of politic prudence—an inadequate reconciliation of the humanitarian instincts of liberal internationalism with the sternly antimoralistic precepts of conservatively inclined (and, except for its particular tragedy-related ethicism, amoral) political realism.

Ultimately centered in the categorical difference between structured even if potential (including nuclear) and unstructured but actual (including terroristic) violence, the ensuing crisis is operationally focused in the difference between statecraft among roughly equipowerful and qualitatively comparably equipped powers and siegecraft engaging diametrically opposite types of parties.

Classic statecraft is, chesslike, a matter of sophisticated moves and countermoves aimed at specific and immediate outcomes with hypothetical, but in principle calculable, medium-term consequences. Such statecraft flourishes qua interstate *politics* in situations of identifiable players (or actors) contending within a clearly articulated setting (or arena). It engages both qualitatively and quantitatively comparable capabilities in a contest over rationally defined and intrinsically manageable stakes. Siegecraft differs radically from this classic battleground of armed diplomacy by its association with more diffuse inter-, sub-, and superstate *relations*. It is evocative of an earlier era's primitively enacted beleaguerment of a vulnerable fortress by an armed horde. A siege's outcome is typically decided by one of the two parties' earlier, or both parties' eventual, decimation by the natural forces of famine or plague, inducing psychic collapse. The issue is less who prevails over whom by a strategic masterstroke than who succumbs first to forces superior to both sides.

Historically associated with the transition from medieval feudalism to statism, siegecraft has a logic of its own that has been resurfacing over statecraft at the point of reversal from statism to an updated corporativist or communitarian, or a backward tribal or ethno-cultural societal, pluralism. The unifying hyphen between the beginning and end of a millennial cycle is siegecraft's association, as a particular technique of warfare, with either a hard-to-overcome military stalemate in a protracted conflict or conversely a hard-to-contain sociopolitical volatility subject to periodic convulsions.

The prime target of a siege is presently an enclave that is more easily definable than its besiegers. The enclave can be called "civilization," provided the term is understood as connoting distinctive technological and institutional attributes and norms of conduct that reflect a particular culture. The besieging or already infiltrated others are implicitly the barbarians, defined by what they value-neutrally are—non-Westerners in terms of advanced technology and organization and particular modes of behavior—and what they are not, or are not necessarily, inferior in terms of objectively construed cultural (i.e., spiritual, artistic, and related) values. Despite the historically correct formulation of the distinction, it will offend conventional hypocrisies. It is, nonetheless, unwittingly conceded in the ultimately testing context of a very special and revealing valuation—that of human life. This value has been driven to historically unprecedented and real politically unsustainable heights inside and with respect to the civilized parts of humanity. It is being radically recalculated downward with respect to humanity's larger remaining part. In the context of man-made military engagements, the near-openly declared exchange rate between American and, say, Iraqi lives is highly unfavorable to the non-Westerners. No higher value is assigned to, say, a Bangladeshi as compared with a Californian life in the context of a nature-made disaster. Nor is this so primarily because of the quantitative ratios of casualties relative to total population in conditions of peace, or due to the qualitative distinction between a friendly and a hostile side in a military context.

In an environment where the prevalence of siegecraft over statecraft is part and parcel of the prevalence of prestatist social forms on the part of present besiegers and poststatist mentalities on the part of the besieged, another distinction becomes pertinent: one between society and community—the former pragmatic-materialist, centered on contract, and the latter organic-normative, based on solidarity without ignoring differentiation by status. When we project such formal definitions against material substance, we discover that the newly salient polarization is not primarily between discrete civilizations. Critical divisions fracture their unity along both vertical and horizontal lines: vertically between polities engaged (qua powers) in alliances across civilizational divides or boundaries; and horizontally within polities between elites and masses, less apt to forge alliances across divides in terms of status than to behave at cross-purposes in terms of needs and interests. This particular division is all the more flagrant if the polity belongs to the category of global have-nots. Relatively more civilized or also cultured elites will propagate there an all the more extreme idealism, the closer is the connection between material distress and governmental incompetence. Coincidentally, the more the barbaric masses are collectively fanaticized, the more ardently its individual members will seek refuge from local misery among the "great satans." Among the global haves, the northern elites become the silent partner of the southern ones when they confuse *their* publics by misconstruing the implied socioeconomic and moral issues in ways that favor misallocation of material and normative resources pertinent to the two kinds of issues.

The resulting international class war cuts through civilizations at a particular level of economic performance different for each civilization. This fact makes nonsense of a pure and simple intercivilizational clash, except insofar as materialism is statistically more prevalent in some civilizations and compensatory idealism predominates in others. Nor does the issue point to an end of history. As an instance of the present's return to earlier phases of world history—the temporal side of the modern international system's passing—the upheaval increases the hazards of the center of history itself passing spatially from one civilization to another. To intimate as much is to suggest that previously experienced world historical phenomena are relevant for the forthcoming world political process with respect to events and situations that extend over a long evolutionary cycle, are instigated by discernible proximate causes, and point toward more or less short- and long-term consequences.

What is the most striking analogue of contemporary migrations that inject a policy focus into diffusely shapeless world politics while raising issues of assimilation of others, revitalization of self, and eventual displacement of an overburdened to an alternative center of survivability after a long period of disorder? It is the predicament of the late (western) Roman Empire, a civilizational center exposed to migrations and infiltrations by culturally alien barbarians pushed from behind by a more numerous or potent populace and attracted by the lure of greater abundance. Thus also present-day migrants west- and north-ward are driven as it were from behind—or, more precisely,

About the Two Cities of Man   37

from within—by a contemporary version of the land-population ratio that, combining overpopulation with underproduction, cannot be stabilized locally.

The latest migrants' uncontrollable influx has been once again aggravating the social crisis of increasingly adversarial allocation of finite resources within the besieged civilization: decreasingly fertile land in postclassic antiquity, decreasingly plentiful low-salaried employment in postindustrial postmodernity. Moreover, the self-generated surge has in both instances been the no longer welcome follow-up to the desired response to an earlier demand: for outsiders to fulfill functions (defense by the barbarian *federati* and menial labor by the so-called guest workers), which the "civilized" populace was no longer disposed to perform because of declining morale in one case and insufficient need or motivation expressed in deteriorating work ethic in the other. Such a parallel with a waning civilization is ominous for the modern West at a time when the center of the state system is passing eastward in space toward Asia. A genuinely geostrategic and geoeconomic confrontation between a West that regressed in time back to late antiquity and early medieval type of societal pluralism and a resurgently statist Asia would update another historical precedent, raising China to the challenging position once occupied by the empire of the Ottomans. A largely justified part of rationalizing the range of actual reasons for the succession would then be inverting the West-flattering modern norm into its historically antecedent opposite, the Eastern powers' self-perception as the civilization superior in all respects except the technological.

What are the late modern-age causes of the differently West-threatening reversions to past eras? A relatively proximate cause of the systemic or real political kind may with some justification be sought in the course and outcome of the First World War, which enlarged the West in terms of mobilizable power without sufficiently compensating for the marginalization of its receding former center. The meaning of this cardinal event is conventionally decided by the insular Anglo-Saxon interpretation of modern history, adopted under the impression of defeat and dependence by Britain's concurrently liberalized French allies and America's German allies. A contrary, continentalist interpretation will instead of celebrating the outcome, stress the cost of a war that, rather than being contained by an early negotiated peace reflecting the military situation's pluses and minuses (on balance favorable to the Central Powers), was being indefinitely prolonged so as to encompass (thanks to decreasingly covert American partisanship) the total victory of the European democracies.

In this perspective, the decisive cause of much of the twentieth-century turmoil is the American barbarians' intrusion into the intra-European balance of power, on a par with the Romans into the Greek and the French into the Italian. The invitation addressed to the United States by the militarily faltering British and French highlights the once again critical difference between particular and more inclusive interests and individual and corporate liberties. As long as the issue was posed between individuals and states, answering it in favor of the state's autonomy was the precondition of a balance of power operating to protect individual powers against hegemony for the ultimate benefit of Europe's emergent civilization as a whole—and incidentally of most Europeans' personal freedoms as well. Calling in the United States misapplied the principle of the state's primacy to the detriment of Europe as an autonomous state system, already sufficiently challenged in emergent world politics to require becoming the next primary corporate entity with a sense of identity.

Not accidentally, this misapplication of priorities laid the basis for catastrophic developments in Germany and Russia, removing the latter as a counterpoise to the former and making it eventually impossible to apply appeasement, construed correctly as a technique of accommodation rather than preemptive capitulation, to the Wilhelmine empire's successor/avenger. The end result for a diminished Europe was the eclipse of a culture-cum-civilization as a corporate power, after it had over many centuries flourished on the strength of successive transfers of preeminence from a power no longer to one already capable of focalizing the process of combining continuity with change. Most directly responsible for the state of things engendered by the mass migrations is in this context the first by-product of America's piecemeal slippage, during and after the last in the consequent chain of worldwide hegemonic wars, into Britain's more self-conscious pretension to rescue others from ills at least partially due to the self-interested continental arbiter because would-be oceanic monopolist: a precipitate dismantling of Europe's colonial dependencies. Insufficiently ready ex-colonies were to be soon, and for some too soon, cast off from the imperial moorings (and the colonial powers' responsibilities) so that they might learn to swim on their own, only for many to start near immediately sinking in the very sea of troubles that keeps projecting ever more would-be escapees from the blessings of sovereign independence onto western and northern shores.

This example of the inextricable connection between inherently manageable central-systemic process and its ultimately uncontrollable peripheral product raises a fundamental question: What should be the relative weight of national and wider, beyond systemic civilizational, interests and is therefore the location of the foremost autonomy to assert and protect? An authoritative answer is not enshrined in a politically correct proposition with sufficient safety to silence the necessary qualifications.

So that we may begin to address the issue of an appropriately nuanced response responsibly, the environment must be correctly perceived for what it is, and is not. It is not in either its totality or its present actuality a crystallized interstate system that permits rational means-ends calculations and is subject to a persistent anxiety recommending (and, at least in principle, requiring) continuous strategic engagement—a constantly alert readiness for involvement even when untranslated into intervention. Likewise largely absent or at least suspended as a result is not only the ripple effect of automatically transmissible disturbances but also the demonstration effect of any particular policy designed to contain an upheaval.

Instead, the global environment exhibits two fundamentally different but interpenetrating elements rather than juxtaposed sectors. One element is an essentially self-sustaining minimum order, shaped by the structures and strategies pertaining to an international system. The second element consists of structurally indeterminate if not wholly amorphous, and behaviorally unpredictable if not integrally chaos-prone, extra- or metapolitical phenomena manifest in socioeconomic, demographic, ethno-cultural and related upheavals. Despite linkages between the discrete elements, the situation does not impose reflexively automatic preemptive or repressive responses. Although the origin of a particular disturbance and the form of a local social pathology do not wholly eliminate the risk of cumulating infection, they definitely confine its scope. Moreover, the absence of an indefinite systemlike chain of reverberations and transmissions minimizes next to the demonstration effect of preventive or suppressive intervention the likelihood of involvement by an actually or potentially hostile party to the systemic sector, acting under the rules of competitive (but inherently orderly) anarchy.

The range of disturbances corresponding to this shape of the environment extends from natural to man-made disasters. Flood or fire or famine are predominantly, if not always solely, natural disasters. Man-made U.S.-Soviet and a comparable past or future classic-systemic or reason-of-state conflict represents the other extreme. An intermediate form obtains when nature, either in the guise of the passional-instinctual side of human nature (former Yugoslavia) or also man's physiological needs (Somalia/Rwanda), directly contributes to sociopolitical disorders. Nothing links the disparate elements of this heterogeneous environment operationally closer together than different kinds of impotence of the civilized-systemic and the barbarian-chaotic actors and a special kind of immunity for the "civilized" sector. The more northern among the Westerners are unable to remove the sources and deal with the immediate consequences of the quasi-nature-made disasters. But they are currently also sheltered by the upheavals' immunity to adversarial rational-strategic exploitation over a historically rare, and in modern times unprecedented, length of anticipable time. The inability necessitates, and the immunity permits, the testing of a wide range of alternative responses.

In determining a response, the first step is to note that the stakes have at once eased and deepened as the identity of the critical polity has expanded: the stakes have eased from immediately threatened military-political security to long-term sociopolitical and economic stability, but simultaneously deepened to meaningful survival; the critical polity has expanded from national to regional communities or major civilizations. These enlarged polities' survival entails—as it has long entailed for established or "civilized" states—nothing more or less than the continuing capacity to function and develop as an autonomous and authentically distinctive entity, sufficiently vital to go on participating in shaping the complex intra- and intercivilizational agendas. After identifying the problem, the next step in ensuring survival is to discriminate among basic strategies. Differences in the situations during and after the Cold War carry over into the dilemma of continuing utility or adaptability of classic Cold War strategies, along the deterrence-defense and devolution-disengagement spectra overlapping in containment.

Direct deterrence lacks the prime conditions of its efficacy, gravity and probability of the cost of undertaking a prohibited initiative, when the cost of a genocidal intertribal killing or interethnic cleansing is no greater to the perpetrator than the cost of flight is to the victim of half man- and half nature-made disasters. Neither rebel against poverty has anything to fear that is plausibly worse than the existing situation—and is, therefore, more compelling than the instinctual (as distinct from rational) response to it. The probability of retaliation is even less than the cost because the hypothetically ultimate target of the local calamity's repercussions is vastly removed, immediately safe, and internally stressed by other problems. Such a provisionally immune party's rational (as distinct from emotional) incentive to block or punish the offending initiatives or incursions will not be more pressing than the desire to avoid a ruinous expenditure of material resources for relieving the sources of the localized pathologies. As a result deterrence will be only indirect and be relegated to measures that are or are designed to be less preventive than punitive, and more demonstratively punitive than commensurately retaliatory. One such measure (witness the confinement of fleeing Cubans and Haitians) is to isolate and confine the migrants at least temporarily in conditions equally or more oppressive than the conditions from which they were escaping; another to proceed against individual perpetrators of (war) crimes such as genocide that cause the flight (witness the even more frustrating attempt to indict Serbian leaders) or organizers of illegal immigration in countries of origin or passage (involving official collusion with the culprits even more glaringly).

The highly limited applicability of indirect deterrence shifts priority from this species of forward defense to direct, frontal or perimeter, defense with incidental risks reminiscent of the Cold War antecedents when constructing extensive antinuclear civilian shelters carried a prohibitive cost to social mores or just societal equanimity. A similar kind of cost now risks being engendered by systematically policed and enforced frontier defenses of a kind that might convert the public ethos of a culturally and materially beleaguered civil society into that of a garrison state. Nor is devolution of roles and responsibilities a remedy that can be effectively exacted from fellow-suffering societies or dependent polities (such as Panama in the case of the Cubans) forced to participate or persuaded to assist in the new kind of warfare, or be secured from multilateral agencies (headed by the United Nations) more adept at upholding peace than preventing any form of war.

Thus, new and different problems abound on all sides. Devolution is now even more difficult to implement via the agencies and less likely to be volunteered by anybody else than it was in connection with the neater issue of geostrategic security. And whereas the new debility of deterrence invigorates defense, the moral-political and organizational problems with static perimeter defense against frontiers-violating migrants, and administrative and legal problems with forward defense against their instigators and exploiters, are sufficient to recommend the more elastic preemptive format. Yet while avoiding moral-political dilemmas, this kind of defense engenders practical-political problems because it entails economically costly efforts and conceptually exacting strategy.

Preemptive defense occurs in depth when it intercepts local disturbances or distresses before their side effects reach the centers of civilization. Inter-great-power strategies that minimize the gestation and exploitation of the disturbances constitute the first line of defense; substantial economic investment is the second line when it is aimed at removing the material sources of distress. Both are preferable to intervention—including humanitarian intervention—that lacks either the grand strategic rationale or the massive resources (witness Rwanda even more than Somalia). Represented as dynamic, such an approach is actually static because it will tend to merely freeze or briefly deactivate the deeper sources of instability. Employing instead substantial economic resources on special occasions and economizing them in all other circumstances, while dealing with local matters as much as possible on the highest great-power level, is the more dynamic application to present circumstances of the Eisenhower-Dulles mix of balanced national budget and massive intervention at places of one's choosing, described at the time as a "new look" relative to the interventionist outlook's Korean implications.

Disengagement may well be said to combine the problems and difficulties peculiar to all of the other particular strategies, rather than cancel any of them. However, it also sidesteps or even helps transcend the problems by moving the all-inclusive dilemma to the fore, where it can be addressed by a rethought and redirected containment. Moreover, as an aspect of overall disengagement, the Eisenhower-Dulles species of preemptive defense is only superficially static. It will prove to have been actually quite elastic when, keeping strategic resources deliberately in reserve most of the time, it allows the autonomous workings of local social processes and real political potencies to restabilize the situation in sufficient depth to reduce materially the cost of an eventual pacificatory or arbitral interposition (a more ideally desirable than actually pursued strategy for Bosnia).

This very dynamic demonstrates the futility of the hardy perennial of ethically self-placating high-minded pragmatism, preventive or prophylactic diplomacy. As a benign substitute for preventive war it shares manifest weaknesses with the favorite of some U.S. military circles at the outset of the Cold War and speculations about a preemptive strike at the conflict's midterm. Preventive diplomacy is no more ethically good by definition than preventive war is morally bad in and of itself. Both suffer from the intellectual arrogance implicit in presuming to anticipate the future and deal with its hypothetical evils in the present. Most crises and all of the truly serious ones cannot be prevented by timely remedial measures internationally any more than intranationally for reasons both theoretical and practical: one, because their specific character will not be known, and two, the disposition to deal with them will not be available or cannot be mobilized before they have become acute. Were this not the case, there would be no revolutions within polities and wars between polities. When crises have surfaced sufficiently, and only then, can they be meaningfully addressed actively or waited out passively—and, when actively addressed, be tackled with a view to either solving the problem or merely containing its scope and repercussions.

In terms, finally, of Cold War's premier strategy, that of containment, other continuities and discrepancies apply. There is now no identifiable outside crisis or threat—and even less a major adversary—of a kind that either can be effectively or need be preemptively contained by available or even knowable means. It is, therefore, more important and also feasible to contain tendencies and temptations peculiar to the self.

To be practiced, first and foremost, is an enlightened self-containment that is resistant to substituting ineffectual and costly interference for materially and politically backed intervention. The prime necessity is to husband economic strength and, if only in the negative sense of popular forbearance for its external exercise, political will. Both are easy to dissipate in an existentially and normatively indeterminate environment. Distinct from the political is the moral side of will, which expresses the self-conscious (while excluding a self-satisfied) sense of rightness of acting or not acting in and on the world. To be refused in support of the practice is, next to dissipation of actual and potential material resource, the relativization of the collective moral self's identity as one worthy of defense. Resistant equally to subversion from the outside and to criminalization from within, this ethical stance is the opposite of either moralism or moralizing that transforms practical restraint expressed in enlightened self-containment into normative self-disempowerment of the community or civilization in the name of individual rights and immunities. At its worst, such disempowerment does more than undermine the ability for not only direct or indirect deterrence and static perimeter or a more dynamic defense. It actually abolishes the possibility of any action or considered inaction arising out of a genuinely free and rational choice in conditions when either form of agenda is permeated by moral ambiguity exceeding the degree commonly inherent in political realities.

In conditions that demand facing up to disasters due to questionable exercise of strategic rationality, passional human nature, or nature as such, a major need is for an ethical stance shaped and applied so as to sustain (next to an effective strategy for intergreat-power processes at the center) the political economy and ecology best suited to phenomena at the periphery. In short, high foreign politics and an austere ethics on the part of a responsible polity are the two levels from which an attempt may be made to contain what is uncontrollable from within at its source. The ecology factor entails a shift from intrusive nurture by the North to an enlarged scope for nature within the South. As for the economy factor, politic self-containment in disbursing material resources will ultimately depend on the capacity to credibly demonstrate moral self-assurance.

A step back from reflexive interventionism to self-containment is presently allowed by the exceptionally nonadversarial condition of the man-made (i.e., interstate systemic) environment. Thus allowed, self-restraint is recommended by the expanding rate of ambiguously natural and man-made disasters and is vindicated by a developing shift in the center of gravity from unintentionally damaging nurture back to self-correcting nature in the physical world and its ethically plausible equivalent in the social universe.

A corresponding focus of policy signals a revolution in the political ecology of world affairs that entails abstention from degrees of interference with human disasters that exceed prudently construed possibilities of even expertly conducted humanitarian assistance. A philosophical precept justifying abstention expresses the ultimately self-punishing hubris attendant on misconceived nurture and overreacting interference with nature, lately demonstrated in America alone by the futility and the environmental and human costs of fighting natural disasters such as large-scale forest fires (California) and major river flooding (the Mississippi). Likewise ineffectual and unintentionally damaging will be humanitarian palliatives of ambiguously man- and nature-made disasters when they prolong and ultimately aggravate the individual and collective suffering they are designed to prevent or at least moderate. It is thus, when years- or decades-enduring safe areas and refugee camps are set up to immediately protect victims of local turbulence physically (when not, in the case of economic refugees, deter them psychologically), but instead actually consign them to ultimately incurable mental atrophy and moral debilitation. Such victims' attempt to adjust to however hard-to-endure local conditions, at however great an immediate personal risk, might well in many instances have a less damaging final result.

Misguidedly applied humanitarian measures and techniques are the international equivalents—and sometimes consequences—of ill-conceived domestic welfare regimes. In one or the other form, such measures implement the tendency for domestic reform programs—from Woodrow Wilson's New Freedom via Franklin Roosevelt's New Deal to Lyndon Johnson's Great Society—to project a spent drive and depleted emotional energy outward onto the international arena, in the mistaken belief of it being more malleable than the national arena.

The ultimate challenge to strategy for the troubled periphery is to employ the findings of a political ecology that has restored nature to equality with nurture so as to foster a political economy intent on breaking the vicious link between ethnicity and poverty. Ethnicity metastasizes from a cultural issue into an acute political problem when it is combined with serious material deficiencies. A frustratingly inadequate material resource is typified from Palestine via Bosnia to parts of Africa by the fixed supply of land, which generates in lieu of sustenance sufficient for all a zero-sum perception of this vital stake and a presumptively winning strategy. Whenever this equation results in subconventionally fought interethnic dissensions, productively cultivable soil has replaced with a vengeance strategically crucial territorial space, the lately downgraded prime stake in conventional international politics. A functional equivalent of hard-to-expand land as the intractable bottleneck in interethnic quarrels is, in the demographic issue of exploding overpopulation, the hard-to-abbreviate medium term in a key developmental process. Not unlike, but even more blatantly than the ethnic, the demographic issue is at its most explosive during the medium term between initiating and consummating the unavoidably long-term process of economic development. That is to say, before heightened material abundance has begun to absorb a consequently declining birthrate and, after redressing, reversed the conflict-breeding land-population ratio in an economy that can productively draw upon the antecedent population increase for positive-sum kinds of activities.

The conclusion is inescapable: only globally diffused material prosperity will over time deactivate the pseudoidealist ethno-nationalist or religio-fundamentalist antitheses to Western materialism as well as the very concrete incentives to massive flights toward materialism's products. Both attenuations are necessary to placate the hostile challengers of a civilization that is resented because it is envied. Only when this has happened will worldwide civil society take sufficiently firm root to begin to engender and experience morally differently precarious benefits. Such a global society's imperfect exemplar, unpredictably altered in the meantime, will then begin to exchange beleaguered stability for assured and potentially beneficent survival—if it still, or again, deserves to thrive.

Insofar as liberal trade policies are both regionally and world-wide the most effective available engine of spreading economic development, any significant protectionist amendment of the liberal stance is not a valid part of conservatively biased isolationist correction of liberal internationalism in politics. Nor is a more than absolutely necessary expenditure on conventional military defense against systemlike threats such a constituent element. Such expenditure carries the unnecessary risk of becoming economically depressant at home (note Eisenhower's part in the original New Look strategy), and the purchased defense risks being geostrategically maladapted to the nature of existing external threats (note Dulles's contribution to the same). The general post-Cold War advantage of economic over military factors has been demonstrated convincingly, because negatively, all the way from Somalia to Bosnia. No amount or kind of military or militarily backed diplomatic interference was capable of making up for the lack of material resource available for and applied to a fundamental recasting of the ethno- and sociopolitical terrain of the upheavals, consigned otherwise to a morally placating but effectively disarmed preventive diplomacy presuming to preempt the role of high foreign politics and problematically high-minded political ethics.

Interrogation II.
A Crisis: Global or National?

The ambiguously positive/negative effects of the growing influx of global escapees on the West's general economy are being inflected toward the negative side by Adam Smith's invisible hand acting through the successful onetime have-nots. They are achieving what most of the West-haters from the Fourth World can only dream of: a reversal of fortunes by means of postcolonial counterinvasion. Lower production costs are the chief weapon of this invasion when they invert the terms of trade from enriching the West economically into decimating it socially. In this underhanded assault by the invisible hand upon the welfare state, a growing army of unemployables in the faltering citadels of prosperity is not so much the shock troops of feasible defense as the avant garde of the casualties created by the so far most successful of the beleaguerments.

When an economic doctrine that requires competition to be free if it is to be fair elevates a special kind of freedom to the pinnacle of also political correctness, it incidentally rules out any single drastic strategy lest self-protection automatically become a prescription for incremental self-destruction. It becomes ever harder for the typical Western politician to retain or recover from a confusingly liberal-conservative platform a sufficient measure of credibility with either Western have-nots or the until recently well-to-do: the former, when, no less demoralized for being subsidized at an increasingly unsustainable cost, they are ever less acceptably challenged for even the less attractive openings on the labor market by their migrant Fourth World counterparts; the latter, when they are deprived of the more attractive employment by market forces favoring the more efficiently, because more cheaply, productive ex-Third World competitors.

The resulting crisis is neither purely national nor primarily global. It is inextricably both and has, moreover, both a social and a technological side. Under the combined pressures, the world is increasingly polarized between two unequally fed, clothed, and sheltered "cities of man"; and so is the late- to postindustrial West, haunted once again by the specter of "two nations" being henceforth permanently installed within decreasingly indivisible republics. This social crisis is aggravated by an internally likewise subdivided—information-expanding and knowledge-reshaping—technological revolution. When this happens, urgent questions arise: What is the direct or indirect relationship between technological and social revolutions? And what about the American protorevolution that either lurks safely behind the so-called Republican revolution while energizing it or might reach beyond its carefully circumscribed scope and depth to what begins to look like West European levels of disruption?

Two distinctions have been suggested so far, each covering actually overlapping differences: between two branches of a technological revolution, and their domestic and international policy-related ramifications.

Within the revolution in telecommunications, the so-called information revolution affects the range and speed of diffusing data and their interpretation. This facet has a sufficient impact on political culture to have an immediate effect on the actual or perceived efficacy of incumbent governments. The associated knowledge revolution affects the ranking or differential salience of particular kinds of information and, consequently, productive skills and professional requisites. It bears on political economy with significance for comparative social utilities. Just as the perception of governmental efficacy and the valuation of social utilities converge in determining societal stability, so too the two revolutions overlap and interact. They do this when the knowledge revolution occasions economic distress for incumbents of traditional (manufacturing and other) forms of employment in favor of possessors of the economically newly creative (manipulative and other) skills; and when the information revolution (that fosters both the vision of a nationwide electronic town meeting and the possibility of its demagogic exploitation) spreads and by diffusing societal disaffections augments and crystallizes the sources of instability.

The immediate social product is politically significant, because both vocalization- and aggregation-capable groups of self-perceived have-nots within the global haves tighten the connection and intensify the interaction between the national and the international planes of the crisis.

The internal crisis is in principle and less certainly in practice susceptible to either conventionally political or more radically revolutionary remedies united in a predesigned, institutionally or extra-institutionally nurtured, solution. The foreign counterparts of the domestic approaches (international organization in lieu of government and war in lieu of revolution) are not comparably equipped to deal with the comparatively lesser speed, intensity, and wide-ranging diffusion and crystallization of the disaffection of the global have-nots across national and civilizational boundaries. When these handicaps are combined, remedy for the global have-nots shifts automatically from nurture to self-correcting nature as the sole, albeit more protracted and tortuous, avenue to correction. This or any other difference does not preclude a likewise protracted, indirect, and hypothetical effect of the presumptively more manageable domestic side of the dual two-cities crisis on its more intractable global side. Nor is the obverse direction of influence ruled out when international trade policies or other cooperative "regimes" delimited regionally (a NAFTA) or globally (a WTO), or a particular foreign policy action (a Gulf War), are explicitly and directly related to the generation of employment at home.

Supposing—a not wholly reliable supposition—that the domestic side of the crisis in the United States can be remedied and resolved by conventional, narrowly political and institutional means, the alternative approach through a social revolution becomes correspondingly redundant in principle and less likely in practice. However, constituent elements of the more drastic approach are none the less latent in the combined effect of the two aspects of the technological revolution—quantity of information and quality of knowledge. The sociopolitical revolution they spawn may be and may long remain confined in a comparatively settled polity such as the United States to intensified pressures for change in the procedural niceties and programmatic messages of a customary (i.e., two-party) political system. But the two-sided technological revolution can nonetheless extend significantly into a potentially explosive link between political culture (subject to informationally diffused disaffection with the political system) and political economy (subject to radically reranked employment opportunities and social utilities).

The knowledge side of the revolution has been represented as the most important new "wave" since the industrial revolution; its information side is, by contrast, the most spectacular advance since the invention of the printing press. It consummates the shift from a tangible medium of communication, the printed page, which connects the inevitably more active author with the unequally more passive because unequally reflective readers, to a multilateral network of comparably active (if not necessarily thoughtful or reflective) communicants through the likes of Internet along the widened two-lane highway. This and other means of expanding the range of information's recipients and accelerating the rate of its diffusion does not automatically enhance the knowledge contents or quality of the exchanges. It does expand, however, the number of participants in a process with correspondingly amplified positive and negative social and political consequences and products.

Ever since the range of participants in the imparting and receiving of information expanded from the monastic scribe and his handwritten artifacts to and beyond Enlightenment elites and their epistolary and pamphleteering exertions, two critical questions have arisen. One, the equation between information and either spiritual or secular illumination and thus information's value for humane culture. Two, the balance of power between the governing and the governed and thus the merit of information in terms of narrowly political culture. Will the expanding access to information extend the capacity of government to deal effectively with social predicaments and enhance, along with this capacity, the moral-political authority of the political class or elite? In principle, a tentatively affirmative answer may apply at the beginning of every stage of the audience's expansion and a governing system's revolutionary or evolutionary mutation. By the same token, the advantage will progressively shift to the political regime's or system's critics and opponents and will have revolutionary implications when the expanding radius of societal malaise has reached the critical mass by way of ramifying economic distress. The typical response of the haves to a thus expressed socioeconomic disaffection of the have-nots will be conservative reaction in support of the established law-based order, further polarizing the situation.

Pending such a progression, is America already in a prerevolutionary situation, which allows, but also necessitates, effective conventional political response, including reapportionment of emphasis on domestic and external political problems? Is, in other words, the United States passing from blessed exceptionality of ever increasing and expanding prosperity to the nether status of a normal polity subject to age-old tribulations including intermittent stagnation? Specifically, is America undergoing this painful experience on the road toward its progressive Europeanization?

America's journey along this line, begun by increases in elite sophistication of various (intellectual-to-gastronomic) kinds, has debouched in the liberal internationalism of the post-World War II era. Europeanization seems now to be reaching a later stage through the mobilization of mass societal disaffection. It may or may not suggest a protorevolutionary situation that anti-internationalist xenophobia, posing as patriotism on the mass level, is on the elite-level matched by a tendency to residential and educational self-segregation: a privileged choice of where to live and how to earn a living—the two residually still-available historic ways of expressing ideal advantages of wealth or status in the era of mass diffusion of traditionally restricted luxuries. Shaping thus near-tangibly the social landscape of the "two cities" means ensuring, if nothing else, physical self-protection by way of self-insulation—a contemporary form of the socially challenged and politically delegitimized ruling class's immemorial flight to country estates from urban centers of populist turmoil.

If all this and more is reminiscent of the Europe of the 1920s and 1930s, the delayed repetition is part of America's parallel journey, extending beyond the return to normalcy after the First World War. Being now, after winning the Cold War, caught up in the fullness of the predicament of a postindustrial society is conversely an unjustly rude awakening for the inhabitants of the "shining city on the hill." Although neither the progression to normality nor the regression from triumph guarantee the continuance of Europe's earlier course and its consequences, the similarities do suggest diminished external efficacy and require greater emphasis on internal remedies. This being so, America's continuing sociopolitical Europeanization (a more substantial and significant process than Europe's cultural Americanization) entails a parallel de-Americanization of Europe's foreign policies (as probably a necessary antecedent to America's progressive disengagement from Europe).

Thus, in regard to both the Fourth World periphery and the Eurasian heartland, the interlocking national and global polarities strengthen the argument for America's foreign policy posture that is apt to preempt the negative (genuinely isolationist and nativist) external ramifications of society's alienation from conventional politics internally. What, if any, contribution to a historically intelligent and intuitively correct response can be forthcoming from the currently prominent or only fashionable technological revolution?

Information does not equal, and its excess may easily impede, access to knowledge—a hard-to-define comprehension of elusive relationships within a synthesizing worldview or sympathetic understanding of any socially or normatively significant phenomenon. This cultural fact is even more obvious than the related economic fact: to wit, that prioritizing a peculiar kind of technologically mediated and enhanced knowledge in terms of both material and ideal rewards is at the root of a sociopolitical predicament lacking an immediately definable solution. Ever more of decreasingly significant information is the declared enemy of intuition. Furthermore, socially disruptive consequences of the newly valued, if not overvalued, kind of knowledge reveal the full societal implications of information's role in the decline of sociopolitical ideologies. Increases in (statistical and other social scientifically produced and prized) information have played a crucial role in negatively affecting the credibility of necessarily if unevenly utopian ideologies. An ideology springs from a central intuition of societal adversity and individual aspirations. It is designed to synthesize a problem and its solution in a rationally plausible or irrationally attractive prescription for action. Consequently, any ideology will be discredited by the accumulation of empirical evidence contrary to its premises and fatal for its promises. Thus also the increase of scientific information (and in this case genuine knowledge) has eroded by way of the positivistic reaction to a differently idealistic speculation the credibility of metaphysical and cosmological systems in philosophy—while the science of physics aims (no more but certainly no less hopefully than does social science?) at the discovery of a unifying principle comparable in role and purpose with the core or root principle that ultimately supports the most complex and abstruse philosophical system.

The absence of a plausible ideology in a crisis situation that has been engendered, or only aggravated, by the knowledge- and information-related revolutions of the postindustrial and post-printing press (or post-Gutenbergian) era slows down the slippage into a true social revolution, indispensably dependent on an ideological rationale. But it also inhibits the formulation and, possibly, implementation of an internally coherent pragmatic policy recipe for a temperate and gradual attenuation of the crisis. The result is a condition that is quite normal for a mature democracy in peacetime: the prevalence of negative press and public opinion for actual government when its performance is projected against the civic ideal; but also the danger that this situation, definable as one of permanent *pre*revolution, may not remain confined in safe, because normal, bounds indefinitely. A foreign policy response to external crisis that is correctly tailored to the degree of the crisis' severity becomes then only one, but not least important, device for managing the risks implicit in the situation.

Discourse III.
About Principles and Practice:
Imperfect Politics and Grand Strategy

Any attempt to relate a grand strategy for Eurasia to pressures from the Fourth World will highlight the international implications of the unevenly complete demise of two domestic utopias: welfare statism, the assault on which has coincided with the fading of the Cold War, and the so-called "real" (displacing a frankly utopian) socialism, which perished with one party to the conflict.

The implications of this sea change for the West cannot be managed by either unprincipled pragmatism-cum-diplomatic formalism in the newly constellated West-East crisis area or humanitarian moralism-cum-institutional multilateralism in the South-North theater. Nor will regionally and globally trading economism as an expression of deeper seated materialism prove adequate. That which is called for instead is a reformulation of the perennial link between realism and idealism that would reflect the diversely altered balances between the state and society and, consequently, between real politics and political economy and ethics in West and East and North and South. Only when these issues have been rethought can conceptual ambiguity be lifted from the existential crisis by a grand strategy that deviates from the internationalist expression of the liberal-progressivist utopia.

America's leadership in this effort is severely strained by insufficient self-consciousness as a historically tested state, a deficiency that is insufficiently made up for by the country's dynamism as a society. Resurfacing after brief submersion by the strategic imperatives of the Cold War, this normative deficit augments the handicaps due to a structurally indeterminate environment and is only potentially remediable by harmonizing the often contrarily expressed complementary attributes of state and society. In this respect, the

United States is at a disadvantage relative to great states such as Russia and China—and Germany and Japan when self-punishing responses to their immediate pasts have yielded to the realization of new opportunities and obligations. Beyond emergent regional trading areas such as the North American Free Trade Association and an obsolete security structure such as the North Atlantic Treaty Organization in its present form, the obvious potential for a differently values-centered community resides in a civilization—Western civilization in its broadest compass and meaning—on two conditions. Consistent with the nature of the statist deficit, one of the conditions is uninhibited reflection on America's past that goes beyond its self-satisfied interpretation. Another condition is partial withdrawal from routinized day-by-day international activism. A measured disengagement alone will create the moral space for the reflection and upgrade the material resource for implementing its conclusions.

This newest of American dilemmas discloses how unfit either the optimism of the end-of-history thesis or the pessimism of the clash-of-civilizations thesis is to provide usable precepts for American foreign policy. Both carefully qualified forecasts lack the requisite part of useful prophecy, a prescription for dealing with either the Eurasian or the Fourth World segment of the more general predicament. A strategy capable of meeting the challenge to move from portents to promise has to start from a safe premise. A useful premise is that viable social organizations are defined by changing areas or orbits of minimally necessary affluence and either allegiance or association. Affluence serves man's physical needs within some form of society, whereas allegiance or association serves the metaphysical need within some kind of "state." When the material and normative requirements are present, they engender a community; when either one is lacking, order dissipates into anarchy.

The task of strategy is to avoid anarchy and promote community within the widest attainable orbit. The millennial trend has been to progressively expand the scope of achievable community in response to politically assimilable increases in organizational or technological efficiencies. If the trend continues, a balance of power among nation-states might plausibly be replaced by an equilibrium among regionally circumscribed liberal economies, associated by virtue of no other -ism than regional patriotism. A benignly self-differentiating reciprocal negation of the major, regionally delimited civilizations could then raise all civilizations to new heights rather than imprison them in a combative stalemate antecedent to a controversial succession. So distant a promise is in keeping with the ambiguous character of contemporary predicaments. The plausibility of the prescription and verisimilitude of the promise depend now more than ever on unifying domestic with foreign politics, neither of which is sufficiently determinate to effectively determine the other. Poststatist pluralism activates deadlocks among socioeconomic or ethno-political factions and rules out determination of coherent foreign policies from within in keeping with the liberal or idealist model. Conversely, the indeterminacy of a heterogeneous global environment impedes the conservative or realist model of foreign policy determination from without. Moreover, when an established order has broken down and outlines of an alternative are hazy, asserting or maintaining an actor's claim to role or status no longer intimates its specific interests with compensating clarity; nor does the uncertainty give rise to a basic foreign policy posture better than controversially calibrated interests do or can on their own.

The ensuing dilemmas are most severe when the prime stakes of politics shift from security of the nation to in-depth stability of a larger order and, beyond both, to the integrity of a surviving civilization. Values move into the determinative vacuum, provided that they are sufficiently embedded in a culture's or polity's historicity to make up for the diminished role of territoriality. When they are not, they cannot correct either the abstract character of values focused on all-encompassing humanity or the all-too-concrete character of interests focused on materiality. Historically processed and affirmed values are not conspicuously at work in American foreign policy. Moreover, the demise of policy-rationalizing ideologies has reinforced the deficiency of real politically impelling structure. When this happens, strategy depends for mental construction on anticipatory imagination of a hypothetical but plausible future. This exercise is uniquely difficult for a country unwilling to see its international history as one embedded in self-seeking ambition as often as in self-denying compassion. When such a country is a long-sheltered island power, it is more than ever at sea when casting about for directions in the sudden absence of not only power- and interest-based guideposts, but also concrete values-related determinants. It is then no more sufficient to rely on spells of ideally others-regarding but real costs-avoiding humanitarianism than to depend on trade-centered economism.

So viewed, America's present predicament is beyond instant remedy by the habitual recourse to self-congratulatory myths that underlay parochially exclusivist isolationism in this country's infancy and have more recently been sublimated into globally interventionist internationalism. An uneven crystallization of internationally serviceable national values can be as destabilizing as the more manifest disparities between power or interests and commitments. Both discrepancies can be best attenuated in the largest possible shared identity capable of compensating politically and culturally for the fading dictates of territoriality while replenishing the spiritual vacancy engendered by the ascent of material utility. If such a frame of reference were to be a civilization, it would be no more easy to define for a multicultural polity such as the United States (or China or Russia) than to translate the promotion and defense of the values a civilization embodies into a foreign policy. Just as the other weakened determinants, so also this particular lack of clarity recommends a respite from aimless activity. Nevertheless, the new significance of values necessitates accommodating altered priorities and procedures in a grand strategy. Fortunately, extending the disposable foreign policy-relevant timetable within a spatially shrinking globe and amid accelerating technological change does not constitute a contradiction. This extension is, rather, a positive way to decelerate the late rush of history so as to prudently avoid its malignant terminus, while profitably deferring its ostensibly benign end.

Revising philosophical and ethical presuppositions to fit actuality is the first step toward a strategic concept linking the central (or Eurasia-centered) contingencies to the peripheral (or Fourth World-related) crisis as tightly as possible. Strategy will produce good history when it is designed to mute the polarization between Western materialism and compensatory Eastern and Southern ideal -isms incarnate in ethnic or religious fundamentalism. To this end, material substance has to be made to coalesce with immaterial spirit in a contrived fusion of productive modern economics with the perennial internal economy of politics—a very special kind of economy that relates the political physics of interacting rival forces in space/time to the tragic poetics of mutually fatal collisions of ostensibly divergent values that, prudently relativized by differences in actors' situations and stages of evolution, emerge plausibly as equally worth promoting and improving upon. A fusion of so diverse elements can be retrieved only from a grand strategy that takes into account the appetites of consumerism (doing duty for the relationships of production in a differently conceived dialectic) but corrects and contains these low politics by high politics. To merit the prefix "high," foreign politics has to be sufficiently grounded in the constants of geography to reenact, in subtly changing ways, the continuities in history. Insofar as it simultaneously incorporates and transcends "low" politics, this higher politics automatically eschews the status of either a mere superstructure of any economic base including that of the free market or a mere extrapolation of domestic political dynamic including that of Western-style democracy.

Implementing this unconventional, statist variety of idealism that interrelates concrete factors with transcendent norms is to oppose a thus dialectically shaped realism to the dichotomy between two materialisms: the vulgar materialism of a prosperous West and the pseudo-scientifically historical materialism of a defunct East. The statist variety of idealism is also diametrically contrary to both the pseudoidealism and the pragmatic utilitarianism of those from the East and South who aspire to speedy integration into Western organisms (from European Union-cum-NATO to NAFTA) with the expectation of being rewarded by instant prosperity, permanent security, and resurrected cultural identity. However, for a philosophic rationale of a grand strategy to be useful practically, it has to be disciplined intellectually by operationally usable precepts. Reformulating the Cold War strategies of deterrence and defense, devolution and disengagement, is a readily available method, although in the (geostrategic West-East) central sector more easily and directly than in the (politico-economic North-South) peripheral sector. The difference is due to the essential continuity between the strategic quandaries that affected U.S. policies toward the Soviet Union on the global plane and their current depression to the regional level. Concession of regional paramountcy at the beginning of the Cold War and of something approaching geopolitical parity more widely as an avenue to enduring stabilization and (Soviet) regime liberalization later on could then be pitted against out-spending or otherwise impelling the objectionable regime into collapse.

Subject to differences in immediate urgency of an issue and a particular regime's attitude toward the United States, identical quandaries reappear regionally and require new assessments more urgently than instant decisions. Should tacit devolution of primary responsibility to, say, Germany as a regional hegemon in East-Central Europe and Russia farther east, Iran in the Islamic world, and China in Asia, endorse the country's regional preeminence? Can an integrating security structure mitigate the paramountcy or will it legitimize the superiority by performing as the respectable medium for its exercise? Or else should a head-on counterbalancing opposition frustrate the ambiguously real or only suspected ambition? Finally, if the radical if not revolutionary approach is to be undertaken, at what acceptable cost to wider stability compared with gradualist evolution?

In view of the unfolding cost of the ostensibly successful one-sided resolution of the global conflict, even retrospect does not provide definitive answers. A highly circumspect wait-and-see attitude is consequently all the more appropriate on the less salient and immediately explosive regional issues. The one certain prerequisite of long-term strategy is ongoing recalculation of the costs and benefits different kinds of defense and disengagement entail for a revised containment formula. This crucial revision is accomplished by a policy that inverts isolation as a condition sought for the adversary into one to be avoided by the self and does the same for mellowing as isolation's presumptive consequence. Pursuing this objective automatically upgrades siegecraft relative to manipulative statecraft also in the Eurasian theater. Especially in this theater, a desirable form of defensive siegecraft sustains morale through evidence of intuitively convincing foreign policies. Siegecraft then ranks above a species of statecraft that progressively dissipates morale and engenders a sense of drift by reducing foreign politics to unavoidably inconclusive formalistic diplomacy among states and to policy-simulating administrative management within pluralistic regional communities.

If only by default, an imaginative grand strategy and the way it is communicated has become the prime medium for injecting a sense of immaterial values and purposes into politics. When the alternative is prostituting values in sectarian fundamentalisms and fanaticisms, politics is in manifest need of restorative renewal, no less in the prosperously postreligious societies of the West than in the economically unsettled postideological Eastern political systems headed by Russia and prominently including China. A foreign policy can be normatively idealist in a manner that allows it to remain geostrategically realist and be historically traditionalist without ceasing to be forward-looking. For the United States, this achievement is hindered by an official rhetoric that fails to reflect reality and a propaganda that does not fit actual policy. A posture problematic with respect to Eurasia becomes also fallacious in regard to the Fourth World when collective self-idealization projects one's many-sided past into a supposedly immutable vocation for performing good works abroad.

Meeting the augmented challenge with reduced resources requires amending traditional realism beyond what is sufficient for the prudential pragmatism of realpolitik in one of the sectors and renouncing the impotent moralism of realpolitik's deniers in the other sector. It does not necessarily entail extending a reasoned correction of an unbounded internationalism to all-out isolationism.

The liberal variety of internationalism, implemented through a pronounced bias in favor of interventionism, has been invalidated as America's foreign policy dogma in all of the doctrine's original precipitants and persisting presuppositions: historic (reaction to Nazi and then Soviet totalitarianism), conceptual (imbrication of all parties and phenomena that automatically penalizes nonintervention by precipitating hostile exploitation or dangerous crystallizations), and economic (worldwide diffusion of sociopolitically liberalizing or even democratizing economic development and growth that is sufficiently rapid to reduce both the aggregate cost of midterm involvements and the likelihood of their open-ended continuance). By contrast, the conservative outlook would economize on both material and psychological resources in exchange for accepting heightened risks. It spurns circumferential management of problems or crises in favor of uncovering a ramifying central principle and trusting a corresponding mechanism. In economics the difference is, say, between imposing wage and price controls and manipulating the money supply as part of mitigating if not mastering the perverse relationship between inflation and growth. The analogous difference in international politics is between trusting the balance of power in its compacted statist or more pluralistically diversified variety and trying to tame power and impose peace by international law and organization.

Currently the central principle is to protect the West without provoking the East. The attendant policy imperative is to safeguard a faltering Russia's European rear as part of enlarging the West so as to secure the "core" West against a frontal advance by China being undertaken with Russia's complicity. The implementing mechanism is a security strategy that balances the dangers of provocation against actual needs for protection. Achieving this optimum in the short run saves material potential and moral resolve for the long run in a considered trade-off between economized resource, downsized role, and acceptably heightened midterm risk.

Such an inherently conservative approach is yet to be converted into an actually conservative U.S. foreign policy. But it can be evolved from upgrading historically evidenced Republican over Democratic strategy biases and policy associations. Accordingly, a post-Cold War "new look" strategy updates post-Korean War anti-interventionism in combination with neo-Eisenhowerian economy (balanced federal budget) and quasi-Dullesian selective intervention at times and places of one's choosing—a component to be presently underwritten by a massive nonmilitary resource and a vastly more preventive than retaliatory rationale. This equivalent of another Republican doctrine, proclaimed by Richard Nixon at Guam and implemented by Vietnamization in another peripheral war, projects into the aftermath of the central conflict the same encouragement for local self-dependence via managed disengagement. Finally, and on the highest strategic plane, Robert Taft's alternative to NATO in the form of a U.S. guarantee reemerges from the Cold War's earliest stage to renewed relevance at a time when the ultimately decisive or, at least, contemporaneously most convincing argument in favor of an integrated alliance—the indispensable psychopolitical effect of deployed American manpower in a dispirited Europe, no longer does or ought to apply in a "new" Europe.

All these ambiguously internationalist-isolationist Republican approaches are presently applicable to both the core issue (immediately involving statecraft toward Russia and its implications for military defense and defense expenditures) and the contextual issue (concerning in the first place siegecraft and its economic connotations). The continuing aim is to preserve vitally critical American reserve power, this world's ultimate fall-back resource to be saved from dissipation for the sake of ensuring its effective deployment as the guarantor of last resort in places and situations where it could do the greatest good. Creating and using such power is directly implicated in the direction of policy attention and priorities. The Grand Old Party's emphasis on Asia, as distinct from the rival party's stress on Europe, is enduringly significant for an offshore insular power doomed to repeatedly redistribute its prime concern between two equally adjoining halves of a potentially overwhelming supercontinent. Reemphasizing the Asian half corresponds currently to another fact of nature recorded in history, the secular gravitation of the sources of power and prosperity from smaller to ever larger bodies of water—from the Mediterranean via the Atlantic to the Pacific. Instead of abiding by this trend, one can continue to adhere to the conception of America as an inherently, rather than from time to time operationally, European power. Doing so, however, mistakes a transiently necessary nurturing device—the temporary implantation of military personnel, presently inherited from a bygone contingency—for a geostrategic constant and an immutable condition of cultural identity.

Denying nature in any way or fashion will make America's pretended Europeanness increasingly costly for the United States and Europe as well. Persisting in the fiction past its utility for both sides does not only divert America from Asia. With more serious immediate consequences it also diverts the western and the eastern Europeans from repositioning themselves productively relative to one another and recentering the continent as a whole in the larger Eurasian and global setting.[6]

It is part of the ultimate unity of politics that the dynamic of succession between two parties has a root cause in the social evolution of each of them. A hostile takeover of a declining party by an ascendant party is made easier when the passage from status to contract, which attends and propels evolution, has been inhibited in or mismanaged by the receding side before either party could enter the kingdom of communal solidarity. This evolutionary sequence applies to the international and intercivilizational arena when America's cherished status as the only remaining global superpower is being superseded by the need for a contract that expresses a grand strategy because it articulates a rationale for American *in*action as well as action.

The clause of the to-be-revised global contract that relates to the Fourth World prohibits indiscriminate engagement for the sake of domestic reconstruction and in the interest of occasional reengagement from strength. The contract's European clause revolves around a relaxation of involvements in the interest of gradual evolution of Europe's unity from latent indigenous strength for the sake of actively to-be-redeployed collective strength. The already apparent U.S.-European policy disagreements are fraught with initially only diplomatic realignments on specific if not also secondary issues (e.g., sanctions against Iraqi or Serbian "aggressors"). A U.S.-wrought remedy against the divisions deepening into a divorce becomes automatically America's reparation for having contributed, prior to and during World War I, to the disunities responsible for Europe's subsequent decline as a power.

Within Europe itself, emphasis on status raises its western half over the eastern half as the prime fountainhead of culture and architect of a civilization presently manifest in the preeminent economy. Replacing conspicuous status with a tacit contract in relations with East-Central Europe means offering a different, but equally appropriate kind of reparation: an economic one for the consequences of the eastern marchlands' developmental retardation, originating in disabling military pressures and despotic oppressions from still farther east. This combination of intercepted pressure and consequent retardation was more than once materially profitable to the presently self-described "core Europe" by diverting it toward and beyond the Atlantic. Also this reparation can be mutually rewarding in due course as an economically rational down payment on the immaterial contribution Europe's cultural and geopolitical marginals are called upon to make, in keeping with their likes' many precedents, to the continent's moral as well as power-political regeneration.

That which is ultimately at stake for all concerned is a foreign politics that offers reciprocal respect rather than one-sided condescension here and now and offers solidarity in lieu of contentiously alternating superiorities down the road. To strive for is a posture that readjusts domestic and foreign politics so as to dissipate the internal manifestations of a pernicious North-South duality that, replacing the provisionally muted East-West polarity, causes one kind of divisions in an America decreasingly able to absorb and assimilate all the wanderers (legal or illegal) toward the statue of not so much liberty as plenty and another and mere severe kind in a Western Europe decreasingly willing to underpin a renascent nationalism with a reinforcement of the regional self rather than with resentments of the cultural others.

An infusion of soul into the physical shell of Europe's body politic from its East is not to be either dispensed with or scoffed at with impunity by a thus strained culture and community. No more will America's polity prosper if, satisfying itself with false moralism, it avoids enriching inborn pragmatism with the more romantically spiritual than practically efficient values of the so-called minorities that represent the South within its borders. Absent the enrichment, even a strategically efficient and normatively sensitive foreign policy will not provide a sufficient tonic for a "society of opportunity." No more will it supply an adequate remedy against viewing "American civilization" as either inherently unworthy or ostensibly sufficient unto itself. An inspirited foreign policy can, however, significantly supplement the miracles of transcension and sublimation of the human predicament traditionally wrought by art and religion as the premier weapons or sheltering walls of culture.

The conservative revolution announced in the Contract with America depends in principle on the underlying philosophy's congruence with social reality and, in practice, on the electoral arithmetic of the number of voters that prefer more of social services or less of the associated tax burden—to begin with as disparate income groups and, when the implications of the revolution have become clearer, as specifically affected individuals. Such practical politics does not adequately take care of the principle unless a domestic rationale for less government (read reduction of the welfare state) carries over into foreign policy. This has not been done either in the original Contract or in its implementation while an initial lack of correspondence risks evolving through a marriage of convenience between domestic ultra-Reaganism and external pseudo-Wilsonism into glaring contradictions between reality and rhetoric.[7]

A commitment to phasing out the incoherence presupposes a supplementary contract between America and the world, one that relates propositions about the present (end-of-century) world and its problems to a revised perception of self ("national identity"). The propositions and the perception will shape the premises and precepts embodied in such a contract's particular stipulations and injunctions.

Impressionistically conveyed in the propositions, the newly complex environment compounds change and continuity on the often contrarily performing levels of scientifically grounded techniques or technologies and societal rituals or pathologies, of mystiques embodied in institutions that constitute civilization and the impulses and instincts that incarnate human nature in the shaping of culture. Their mutual conditioning is as much part of the energetic motor behind evolution as their momentary confluence is of evolution's normative-cum-existential matrix. Inscribed in history, this process is driven by the mechanism of particular conflicts and disclosed in specific manifestations of change. A plausible polarity around which to presently order analysis of the process on the doctrinal or philosophical level is that between conservatism and liberalism. Its correspondence with the polarity between statism and societal pluralism on the structural and normative levels is operationally concertized in the schism between continental(-military) and insular(-maritime/mercantile) types of power and polities.

To what precepts do these perceptions and propositions point as relevant for America's new contract with foreign policy significance?

1. Neither pure individualism as the core-value of economics-centered (contemporary Anglo-American) conservatism nor all-out (U.S.) isolationism or (British) Euroskeptic nationalism as its extreme international corollary can provide an answer to contemporary crises any more or better than their liberal progressivist if not utopian alternatives have been able to on the strength of meanwhile invalidated assumptions. Elements of traditional continental European (and Tory paternalist) types of conservatism must be, therefore, injected into the extravagant extremes of narrowly market-oriented conservatism if it is to reactivate the perception of society as an organism with attendant solidarities and of the state as a values-rich agent of real politically mediated historicities.

   An authentically mature postexceptionalist America is correspondingly challenged to master the policy nuances implicit in simultaneously resuscitating and moderating the rigors of renascent nineteenth-century social Darwinism of its adolescence in both domestic and foreign politics. The United States can do so when, having assimilated the still viable features of traditional conservatism in principle, it has reactivated the emphases prominent in Republican foreign politics from before World War I (emphasis on Asia) and from during the Cold War (emphasis on other parties' self-reliance).

2. The future of world politics is stretched between communitarian pluralism in the West and locally preserved or incrementally resurgent statism in the East. These structures (and associated values) are projected strategically into more or less orderly and pacific reranking, as to their comparative salience, of primarily insular-maritime and continental-military powers.

   Conjointly and consistently with this general given, the future depends on either the reemergence or continuing absence of a claim to old-fashioned—actually constraining if not also coercive—hegemony and on the eventual claimant's identity. This type of hegemony was historically associated with or attributed to continental states. A U.S. strategy shaped to deal with both possibilities from the position of either reserved or restored strength requires prudently watchful prior disengagement from a materially and psychologically insufficiently supported preeminence short of hegemony—a posture historically appropriated by insular powers.

   In the relatively short run, a measure of detachment will diminish the malignant effect of America's lack of a society-transcending conception of the state on foreign policy until the consequent inability to properly assess and address differently constituted major powers has been corrected. Such powers' propensity to draw on the state idea's historic associations has been currently reenergized by the demise of substitute ideologies, previously countered with relative ease by an inherently superior or merely more widely attractive American ideology.

Over the longer run, qualified U.S. disengagement is best suited to foster the communitarian variety of the pluralist alternative to statism's bias toward military-political hegemony as a substitute for unattainable parity with the insular societies' economic hegemony. Disengagement forecloses any action apt to reprecipitate this classic continental option into action detrimental to maritime-mercantile dispositions. A disengaged America has less reason to posit the continental-hegemonial option as likely or inevitable in principle and presumptively latent in any one power in practice. Moreover, eschewing provocation of putatively hostile forces, disguised as preemption, in favor of calculated inaction from a position of recovering strength translates automatically into the emergence of new, or rehabilitation of previously stunted, non-American capabilities. Blending the negative or preventative with the positive and creative features within a correspondingly articulated general strategy is the manageable task of a strategically sophisticated diplomacy. This is the external equivalent of a comparable blend of outright reductions and rational improvements in domestic social welfare policies intended to restimulate individual self-reliance without denying either community creative interdependence or community supportive solidarity.

3. Managing the continental Eurasian core of the world system centered on the German-Russian-Chinese trio through an internally coherent domestic/foreign grand strategy is the only readily available means of constraining the immediately disruptive sociopolitical and progressively debilitating cultural manifestations of the contextual South-North issue, centered on mass population migrations. Absent a strategy that would fit this problem directly, statecraft among major (in technological-organizational terms civilized) powers becomes determining. It assumes the role of maneuvers by main armies in inconclusive siegecraft, oriented toward relieving the besieged party and foreclosing the addition of previously lacking mass to the besiegers.

The alternative to the beleaguered West's timely relief is an eventual and then more determined resort to the strategies and techniques applied during the Cold War, centered on frontal defense and forceful deterrence. Such strategies would reflect a siege mentality that exceeded the measured revision of the ethical and cultural political dimensions of the North-South cleavage necessarily and usefully implied in any

About Principles and Practice 65

reconsideration of the many implications of the cleavage and the alternative methods of addressing it.

4. The contemporary salience of Russia at the center of Eurasia extends in this overall perspective beyond the country's intrinsic importance and capacity to aggravate the northward with expanded westward population migrations. In the ultimately decisive geostrategic theater, the way the West in general and the United States in particular handles Russia and adjusts to the effect of alternative approaches on Russia is the only immediately available method of significantly affecting the evolving posture of China. The United States' attitude toward Russia's critically important relations with Germany is coincidentally the principal test of America's willingness to modulate its involvement in Europe so as to engage itself more effectively in Asia, halting thus the uncontrolled present drift into the opposite allocation of diminished resources.

5. A strategy of the United States for the West becomes grand when it attends to dilemmas of the present and desiderata for the future—and is capable of forestalling a continuing deterioration of the moral and real political environment. A revision of and response to a range of interconnected sociopolitical trends and phenomena will only include otherwise inertially overemphasized issues of military security and overtly active local breakdowns of either security or stability. A grand strategy will relocate the various facets of crisis in a unifying focus on both the internation and the intrastate or intrasocietal plane in regard to a genuinely *political* economy; will reconnect spontaneous dynamics, as distinct from nurturing designs, with the workings of nature in a revised political ecology; and will consequently renounce attempts to transcend politics while defying human nature in societal pseudorevolutions. Attributed to more genuinely revolutionary new technologies or devices of organization, these "revolutions" can be conservative or liberal. But only the self-consciously progressivist ones among them proclaim a radically new morality of a universally expanded compassion, liable to prove ineffectual if not ultimately dehumanizing in particular cases and applications.

6. Insufficiently functional late-evolutionary features of specifically Western civilization have been taking root within a historically minuscule, variably calculable period of time under the pressure of an excessively ideologized contention with antagonistic power systems and alternative societal utopias. This happened within a spatially confined island of material prosperity and psychopolitical lassitude in defiance of both multimillennial recorded history of mankind and the millennial story of the Eurocentric state system, illustrative of the psychological and

operational laws driving politics. The futility of denying so persistent a background is made worse when diplomatic routines lack a geostrategic vision consistent with the accessible degree of the historical background's melioration. This dysfunction is, however, only one and not the profoundest manifestation of the contemporary predicament, which was allowed to deepen because of the West's unwillingness to confront truths offensive to conventional moral prejudices.

The need and possibly the urgency to align the American perception of self with propositions about the world creates space for rethinking national identity into greater consonance with historical reality revealed in the delayed consequences of past American performance.

A plausible polarity around which to order a revised self-perception is the polarity between comparatively unitary continental statism and insular societal pluralism, both of which are concurrently and continuously operative in the environment and its evolution. A revised self-perception effective in policy will de-idealize or de-glorify insular societal identity conjointly with de-criminalizing or de-anathemizing continental statist attributes. It will consequently amend a neoliberal/neoconservative values system anchored primarily if not only in economics with traditionally conservative/historicist postulates sensitive to social ethics and pertinent to geopolitics. Translating the revision into the more complicated mind-set creates a more complex and, therefore, more mature national self, one that corresponds to the more complex (statist-pluralist) structure of any conceivable global order of the future and the order's relation to the equally complex structure of (both political and economic) individual and corporate freedoms.

A resolution might thus be found to the internal ambiguities, if not contradictions, in the current Anglo-American attitude toward the state. Its normative demotion or de facto nonrecognition is attended by a two-part attempt: to combine economic liberalism with sociocultural conservatism and law-and-order statism, and to effect this realignment in variously accented and terminologically labeled combinations of the various -isms.

In the specifically American (and to a lesser degree British) case, the moral authority of the state, conceived as and reduced to a machinery of governance—renamed "federal government" in domestic and "nation" in foreign affairs—is weak to begin with. It is further weakened by the liberal strain's bias toward reducing regulation of free-market economic turbulence in the name of (individual) freedom. But the state is expected to remain strong, or to be made still stronger, for its role in containing if not repressing physical violence. Such violence, when aimed at societal order, is putatively grounded in deviations from traditional societal norms and values; when targeted at world order directly, the use of force is conversely attributed to retrogression from modern if not post-modernist norms and practices.

In both domestic and international arenas, the ideal policy response and hard-to-attain objective is consequently divided between interventionism (to remove obstacles to economic freedom and control violent challenges to order) and non- or anti-interventionism (to minimize artificial distortions of spontaneities that actually create societal stability—and thus a necessary condition of a minimum of political freedom—through wealth creation at home and, occasionally, war abroad). Actually, the inner cleavage between weak and strong state within liberal (neo)conservatism can be muted somewhat, even if not mended, in a compound of interventionism and noninterventionism. Contriving the correct mix in low domestic and economic politics is, however, nothing compared with dealing with the related dilemmas in high foreign politics. This is so, among other reasons, because the factors of (free) economic turbulence and (disorder-creating) physical violence assume a different standing within and in the relations between insular and continental polities.

The insular-mercantile/maritime principle and policy point unambiguously toward (forcible) intervention against violence as one prone to interfere with, if not block, economic processes connected with free trading specifically and the free market generally. This is the self-interested material basis for the most humanitarian of interventionism. The principle and policy are less unequivocal from the different vantage point of continental statism. Concern with economic/material resource is connected therein directly to its military-political context and only by way of the balance-of-power dynamic to the global economic process and trading system. Intervention against extraneous violence, or its conditional tolerance, will be assessed according to a particular intervention's potential for draining (or else relatively augmenting) national material resources and other capabilities in the more immediately critical arena and agenda.

The more different American polity's attitude and policy's relation is to intervention at home and internationally, the more this will confuse a general strategy committed to encompassing both arenas. Minimizing the confusion is necessary to fit the United States for leadership of a civilization such as the Western, which, comprising both the statist and the pluralist elements and the continentalist and insularist attitudes, otherwise continues to be dangerously split along the lines of a Euro-Anglo/American dichotomy. Only when an adjustment has been accomplished in the civilization's identity as an enlarged polity, and in its capacity as a power, will it overcome Euro-American and West- and East-European (Russian) differentials as well as divisions within the multicultural United States itself. Adapting American national identity to these differentials and divisions will incidentally equip this country to lead this same civilization as the framework of culture and integrator of both of the complementary attributes of creative power.

 A pragmatic utilitarianism that is unable to enrich itself by assimilating the emotively spiritualist "southern" (Afro-Hispanic) and the disciplinary statist "oriental" (Asian-Arabic) value systems is unlikely to prosper. It will foster instead a mere juxtaposition of hyphenated American minorities and a culturally undefined abstraction, the residual majority. A contrarily very concrete friction will continue to be concealed only superficially by societal taboos and extra-legal sanctions, expected to police deviations from the declaratory civic ideal sufficiently to contain the frictions' impact this side of irreparable disruption. Conversely, integrating the spiritual attribute of the statist factor into the American self by means of society's intercultural dialectic will promote a unifying political nationhood and, thanks to it, an effective U.S. role in the long-term dialectic between major civilizations qua aggregate powers or enlarged polities. In the interim, even a real political stalemate as an avenue to eventual restabilization overshadows the alternative of destructively contentious politics of succession.

Interrogation III.
A Contract: With Self or the World?

The particulars of a reexamined and revised self-perception (constituting national identity) can be transposed into stipulations and articles in America's virtual new contract with itself, psychopolitically antecedent to and real politically preconditional of an objectively effective and subjectively enforceable contract with the world.

A. Commitments and Stipulations Concerning "Self"

  1. *In re polity*: review the latest acute, post-Myrdalian American dilemma as part of facing up to and resolving the contradiction between an appeal to (free market-cum-democracy type of) universalism, as the foundation of an otherwise faltering global leadership, and insistence on cultural-political exceptionalism. Basic to this operational dilemma is the failure of a multicultural society (or multiculturalism as its dominant precept) to engender a sense of unifying political nationhood, aggravating the newly significant deficit: a lacking sense of statehood as a historically continuous ideal entity distinct from civil society. Responding to geostrategically significant realities, this sense will be reshaped to suggest a basic external posture in an environment once again provisionally much too void of sufficiently determinate structure to determine policies pragmatically.

  2. *In re performance*: review objectively and, therefore, critically past national performance in the chain of wars and conflicts initiated by World War I in light of the positive and negative consequences of U.S. interventions as compared with self-restraint short of self-isolation. This review will imply willingness to revise an inertial insistence on America's status as the one and only superpower in favor of a

contract-type relationship with the world based on individual responsibilities and mutual reciprocities as prerequisites of genuine solidarity.
3. *In re basic posture*: reconsider the governing geopolitical mindset conservatively with a view to adapting interventionism to conditions that invalidate many or most of the historic precipitants and conceptual and economic premises underlying liberal internationalism. Central to such an isolationist correction will be the disposition to reassess the gravity of risks immediately enhanced by nonintervention. Are these risks more or less manageable inherently or just presently when they are compared with hard to assess and address dangers from overzealous interventionism? Central to this reassessment is the inescapable trade-off between political risks assumed through inaction and the material and psychological resources expended in efforts to defer the risks indefinitely if not eliminate them completely.
4. *In re specific policies*: commit America to strategies that reequilibrate the demands and priorities of domestic and foreign politics, for the time being in favor of internal reform and rebuilding. Implement this revision, because it is in keeping with an increased potential of regional disorders for self-stabilization and the lessened capacity for their adverse exploitation by a major power. This state of things is, consequently, contrary to combining domestic social Darwinism with solicitously internationalist Wilsonism in policies coupling less internal government with undiminished appetite to manage, if not in effect govern, the world.
5. *In re general philosophy*: reevaluate prevailing canons and injunctions of political ethics, economy, and ecology (re-elevating nature over nurture) so as to enhance the conformity of national philosophy with the universal of the inner economy of politics (its physics of interacting forces and tragic poetics of conflicting values). This peculiar kind of economy opposes a normatively constrained social Darwinism/naturalism to incoherent combinations of moralism with materialism, currently prone more than ever to substitute technologically expanded information for historically informed intuition in foreign policies.

Revising American self-perception, codified in a new contract with self, along these lines will bring national identity into closer conformity with the premises supportive of America's new contract with the world and the precepts embodied in its stipulations.

B. Premises Supporting a New Contract with the World
1. *Global matters*: The West finds itself at a secular turning point toward the latest social Darwinian (realistic or naturalistic) correction of

utopian meliorism or perfectionism in social affairs. This correction marks a turning away from the stance foreshadowed by the ideological turmoil preceding World War I and culminating after that war's aggravated sequel. Such new departures occur typically in a trough between peaks of international crises, including hot and cold wars. This latest trough and concomitant change of direction coincide with a break in the millennial development of the Eurocentric state system and a halt in the secular ascent of the Western civilization. The internationally most critical recent decades are those between 1935 and 1985, the beginning of serious Nazi and the virtual end of the Soviet totalitarian-cum-hegemonical challenges; the critical "century" extends from the 1890s to the 1990s.

2. *American matters*: The immediately antecedent fifty years crucial for the United States internally extend from the end of World War II to the electoral triumph of the recipe for a Republican revolution. The terminated period was one marked by attempts at sociopolitical melioration and transformation of intercultural relations, linked to two different kinds of war as the reward for parts played in securing victory in the hot war and a weapon for achieving victory in its cold continuance. The social aspect of the welfare state's campaign against roots of domestic instability was the ideological response to promises of rival socialism on the East-West axis; the civil-rights side of the fight against racial discrimination was a response to the salience of the South-North issue (or contest over the Third World) as the seemingly decisive stake at a seemingly decisive moment in the East-West conflict.

3. *Generic factors*: The present revision of welfare statism in America (and to different degrees elsewhere in the West) favors a reversion to individualism. Yet, however boosted by the defeat of the two totalitarian collectivisms, victorious individualism neither need nor can dispense with a form of corporate consciousness that humanizes individualism by drafts on increased national wealth out of regard for enhanced societal sensibilities. Due to the economic product of the classical and the ethical side of reformist liberalism, this easement is available for moderating the conservative reaction to reformism's slippage into utopianism, while the easement's actual scope and manifestations depend on the relation yet to emerge between the domestic and the international aspects of the attendant revolution. Coordination of such a revolution's two aspects is not most important in the interest of academic consistency in guiding principles because it inheres in real politically significant interlocks. One bears on the

finite material capabilities to be redistributed between the two arenas; another on the political responsibilities to be readjusted to present capabilities among the main actors in the international arena; and yet another on the contribution foreign politics can or must make to the values-centered normative foundation of the advertised domestic revolution in the interest of an authentic conservative restoration.

C. Understandings Implicit in the Contract
1. Acknowledgment of *America's performance* in the Cold War and this country's subsequent constraints on material and psychopolitical resources as the basis for complementary self-dependence and more symmetric interdependence.
2. Recognition of the new *post-Cold War environment* as one of structural ambiguity or indeterminacy relative to both statism and communitarian pluralism, acute and latent crisis segmentation, and alternate (security/stability/survival) stakes on the South-North plane (acute global class war situation) and the East-West plane (latent intergreat-power competition and intercivilizational dialectic).
3. Acceptance of implications of articles 1 and 2 in favor of correcting resorts to systematized *nurture* (institutionalized utopianism) with equal appeal to and increased reliance on *nature* (spontaneous instincts and tendencies underlying realism) in foreign politics. Shared understanding of the consequently enhanced salience of siegecraft (comparative endurance of shared adversities) over would-be progressively reformist statecraft (humanitarian multilateral internationalism). Proximate rather than only ultimate reliance on individual and consensually coordinated self-help regionally in real political statecraft, warranting an isolationist correction of U.S. interventionism globally
4. Factually negotiated *revision of (U.S.) Cold War strategies* (defense, deterrence, devolution, disengagement—containment), tentatively on the South-North axis (population migrations) and more effectively or meaningfully on the West-East axis (regional geopolitical issues, replicating global Cold War issues).
5. Consequently altered priorities and emphases in *specific policies*: in Europe/Eurasia, between essentially municipal EU-type politics and inertially NATO-related military security politics, and the geostrategy of the emergent continental German-Russian-Chinese triangle; in Asia, between a replication of either the European Union model in a politico-economic or the North Atlantic Alliance model in a military-political Asian-Pacific equivalent, and not only the recognition of but also gradual adaptation to the geostrategic centrality of China (liable to be shaped by Russo-German entente or alienation and this European

alternative's global repercussions via feedbacks from and effects on the United States and Japan directly and immediately and India indirectly and eventually); and in the Fourth World, between deepening repercussions from compensatory idealism (religious fundamentalism and cultural ethnonationalism) and real progress toward positive values-upholding orderly statism (effective, including forcible, state building or rebuilding) away from chaotic pluralism in the direction of such pluralism's regional community-type institutionalization.
  6. Recalculation of the utility of expending material *resources* as compared with incurring political-military *risks* and accepting a redistribution of *roles*, with implications for the specific shape of an actual security architecture/organization (one continuing to implement static perimeter defense or changing to the more elastic in-depth or forward defense) and for comparative salience of institutionalized military-security organization and promotion of evolutionary stability by political means.

D. Key Strategy-Relevant Aspects and Potential Benefits
  1. *Basic precept* and revision: reaffirmation of the link between domestic politics (resuscitated individualism contained by some form of communalism) and foreign politics (a sufficient degree of conservative retrenchment to correct liberal exuberance), qualifying both types of return to social Darwinism by revitalizing the basis for economically and psychologically viable solidarity.
  2. *Grand-strategic priority*: assurance of necessary protection against, without provocation of, a hypothetical future would-be hegemonic power, by means of preserving national capability and stimulating the rise of new or resurgence of existing friendly or allied forces.
  3. *Single-power focus*: respect for Russia's present or forthcoming salience on the Eurasian issue (and secondarily on the population migrations-related Fourth World issue), conceded or denied through attitudes toward the enlargement of NATO or its replacement by an alternative security architecture.
  4. High versus low *politics differentiation*: revival, through revision, of traditional uses of high foreign politics on the core (Eurasian) and the contextual (Fourth World) crisis issues in ways that combine negative (avoidance) with positive (promotion) aspects and objects of grand strategy, but differentiate high foreign policy from the low domestic and international economic politics driven by the assumption of an automatic link between economic development and political evolution and institutionalized by progressive multilateralization of formal diplomatic procedures.

5. Basic *posture revision*: acceptance of immediate and visible costs in exchange for the benefits accruing from a deliberately managed U.S. resignation from world leadership necessary for reconstruction at home, reactivation of newly capable parties abroad, and either regeneration of the international system or its replacement by an alternative type of order. Disposition to abdicate will in the first phase be either documented or denied through U.S. attitude toward the Russo-German relationship, testing America's readiness for devolution in Europe and the transfer of emphasis to non-European (including Asian) issues for the sake of an equal and therefore effective Euro-American partnership.

6. Basic *philosophy alteration*: incremental mitigation of the post-Myrdalian American dilemma and its consequences. Requires readiness to substitute for the inadequately internalized idea of the state the ideal goal of a regenerated Western civilization, capable of entering creatively an intensified dialectic (as distinct from withstanding the "clash") between the major civilizations by means of normatively complementing civil society, undergirding pluralism, and counteracting pluralism-related utilitarian materialism.

All of the above stipulations are contingent in that they reflect a particular analysis of the present environment and appreciation of the related predicament. Insofar as the stipulations also embody a promise, they are potentially constituent of an order that would weigh individual freedoms and rights against obligations and equitably shared responsibilities, and national interests against systemic or civilizational interests. The proposed contract's stipulations are consequently problematic in that they both precede (are intended to promote) and presuppose (are contingent on partial presence of) comity. Consistent with this ambiguity, the contract's relation to conflict is no more definite or cast in stone: normative acceptance of conflict and its operational inclusion (as an expression of freedom) in actual politics is seen as a practicable pathway to its mitigation (as an element of order). Both of these ambiguities characterize the contract as an instrument of dynamic transition rather than static definition, combining change with continuity and transformation with conservation. As a consequence, the contract both expresses and is intended to expedite the passage from the rights and obligations of a hierarchical order based on status—itself founded in unequal past acquisitions and present assets—to the costs and benefits of more nearly egalitarian solidarity based on affinities and expressed in comparable degrees of community-constituting association or allegiance. All in all, the contract—and the contract-stage in societal evolution—enlarges the space for self-dependent individuality and coordinate responsibility, legitimately manifested in either conflict or community. It effects this enlargement in the interest of change (progress) and continuity (tradition) as the twin constituents of in-depth stability.

Discourse IV.
From Present to Future: Predicaments and Prophecy

The Cold War polarized world politics, but did not produce a global state system. After failing to institutionalize a co-imperial peace on the basis of a military-technologically founded stability consolidated by diplomacy, this conflict bequeathed to world politics the necessity to restabilize itself spontaneously from within its very heterogeneity. By the same token, after one of the contenders had laid more ably than any world power in memory the foundations for the reconstruction of a world endangered by the upheavals of the now departing century, the time has come for America to let go and allow the world to start reconstructing itself on its own in large part and in many of its parts.

Nothing is more certain to undo the United States' historic merit than to continue encouraging others to depend upon it for direction and salvation, only to fail to deliver on the implied pledge at some future decisive moment. A mere possibility of this happening is sufficient to mislead—its actual occurrence certain to betray—all those who had been previously denied the right and indirectly the capacity to depend, not only ultimately but also firstly, upon themselves. Always true, this precept is truer than ever at a time when immediately available American strength and prospectively acute or instantly removable threats have declined in tandem. A U.S. foreign policy that implements the national purpose in conjunction with meeting the world's real needs is one less exalted than the posture proffered by liberal internationalism and will be less restricted than is implied in isolationist corrections offered so far by its conservative critics. A strategy that wisely subordinates instant security to in-depth stability in order to ensure long-term survival will respect a range of internal consistencies, headed by congruence between domestic and foreign politics. This consistency is foremost, because it ultimately determines the relationships and priorities between military and political initiatives and the material and societal support for either. By contrast, inconsistency prevails when individualism as the core value in the dominant economic facet of contemporary Anglo-American conservatism would effectively or finally dissolve conservatism's traditional connection with social concerns intranationally, while an isolationist correction of Anglo-American liberalism became wholly devoid of international solidarity.

The critical distinction within the conservative worldview is between traditional, continental European and British Tory, conservatism with its corporate attributes, and the contemporary Thatcherite-Reaganite/Gingrichian individualistic variety. This distinction is not erased but is obfuscated by the association of individualist features in capitalist economics with collectivist features in populist cultural politics, be they of the nationalistic variety in British Euroskepticism or the familistic variety in religiously propelled right-wing Americanism. The latest version of American conservatism merely extends this contradiction outward when a pretension—to shore up late-mature America's declining capacity for conventional foreign-policy leadership by the universalism of the market—is conjugated with the increasingly juvenile-looking conceit of cultural-political exceptionalism. A U.S. strategy that has become at some point seriously committed to the survival of Western civilization will have to integrate into a trans-Atlantic vision the constitutive primacy of a European culture that had spread out from its native trunk into indigenously modified and thus partially inauthentic as well as potentially innovative far-western (i.e., American) and far-eastern (i.e., Russian) offshoots. This culture depends now for yet another revitalization on its materially deprived but psychologically reborn eastern offshoots' fragile capacity to withstand the corrupting inversion of erstwhile naive enthusiasms into the crudest of Europe's latter-day materialisms.

So inclusively defined but also extensively vulnerable a Western civilization is in terms of policy the power called upon to both complement and protect the inner resources of so multi-faceted a culture. Centered geopolitically and geoeconomically in the United States as a link between Western (Atlantic) and Eastern (Pacific) Hemispheres, and extending critically to the continental European promontory of Eurasia, this civilization is a compound of material goods and immaterial values between which it historically refused to choose. However weakened, the ensuing immemorial tension and problematic relation can usefully continue under American political patronage provided this burden and privilege is not employed to inhibit a crucial partnership—between Germany as the link between Western and Eastern Europe and Russia as simultaneously a link and the *limes* between Europe and Asia. Any policy that clings to solitary U.S. patronage to the detriment of that partnership is implicitly hostile to Russia and will be inevitably perceived as such by any Russian regime looking for domestic authority and concerned about international prestige. Such policy is, consequently, inimical to the cohesion of Europe and the unity of the West. Moreover, the policy will ultimately fail to achieve its immediate purpose of forestalling the diminution of America's role, implicit in any devolution of responsibilities, when change of policy priorities has become finally necessary for material or psychopolitical reasons.

Prior to World War I, the British staged an elaborate diplomatic effort to avoid paying the price of devolution in ways advantageous to Germany. The consequences of misdirecting disengagement with discreet but ultimately decisive American encouragement redounded to Europe's immediate and Britain's eventual detriment. A repetition of this scenario in relation to Russia will fare no better if now staged by the United States on its own behalf. Mismanaged devolution will only aggravate the likewise habitual consequence of a major power's defeat, the progressively surfacing competition among the victors for a privileged rapprochement with the reconstituted loser. When the predictable rivalry will have gotten fully under way, as it had in favor of France after the Napoleonic wars and of Russia after the Crimean War, one thing will become clear about policies designed more or less consciously to forestall competition over who will pull Russia westward without making it part of the West. Such policies will have actually pushed Russia eastward to the prejudice of everybody except perhaps a power belonging to another civilization.

Even as it goes on flourishing economically, an only marginally expanded little Europe can, and more than likely will, continue to stagnate politically as America's strategic protégé. A greater Europe can again conversely become an equally West-constituting power that complements and enhances the identity of its so-called core as a freely and mostly fairly competing commercial polity. If, like the Italy of Cavour and Mazzini, Europe *fara da se* in the image of de Gaulle as well as Jean Monnet, a compensating U.S. reemphasis of Asia will reactivate America's pre- and immediately post-World War I orientation. This reemphasis will complement a matching deemphasis of Asia in favor of Europe by Russian Eurasianists, creating a basis for U.S.-Russian concert (as distinct from anti-China coalition) in the Far East generally and within an Asian-Pacific security structure specifically.

America's partial disengagement in Europe is nothing more and nothing less than an adjustment to post-Cold War realities and a readjustment of post-Cold-War priorities. It expresses a species of negative continuity with disengagement's advocacy at the height of the conflict. Whereas this strategy

80   Discourse IV

was then supposed to set off a perversely Europeanist because inherently oriental despotic Soviet Russia's return eastward toward Asia, its present object is to pull a hesitant protodemocratic Russia westward. For the United States to become simultaneously—and conjointly with something like an Eastern Locarno—only the last-resort, and meanwhile free and independent, guarantor in Europe would be the opposite of expelling America from Europe. An indispensable guarantee would automatically maximize a species of remote control over the main outlines of Europe's long-term evolution while minimizing the costs of micromanaging Europe on a day-by-day basis and on a par with too many places outside Europe. The related choice for *Zwischeneuropa* is between being returned to the status of a forward glacis of a narrow West against Russia in the rear of Germany and escaping the attendant jeopardy. The decision ought to be easy when the promise of protection by NATO spells provocation of a Russia left outside it; when an eventual failure to implement the promise (be it a pledge made explicitly in a treaty or implied in ambivalent policy) is only too likely to join a long series of Western defaults extending (when only contemporary history is taken into account) from 1938 to 1968. In light of such a dim record, there is much to be said for the in-between Europeans connecting Russia with Germany and through Germany with Europe rather than separating Russia from Europe and making Europe permanently dependent on an increasingly burdened and cumulatively distracted America.

The twilight of Greece resembled the present when it was marked by an uneven weakening of both the continental and the insular antagonists in a great and prolonged conflict. The debilitations created space for second-degree regional quasi-empires, be they politico-economically liberalized (such as the second Athenian empire, equaling a fourth German and second Japanese) or narrowly based military (Theban, equated by locally limited Russian or Chinese). The real question, however, concerned then as it does now the likelihood and, were it to materialize, the identity of the next continentwide hegemon. This could be one expanding aggressively from a depleted and divided state system's marchlands (then Macedon or now eventually a neo-Czarist Russia in Russia's second and final bid, paralleling France's under Napoleon following Louis XIV and Germany's under Hitler following William II) or one sucked in from afar by the state system's or civilization's internal discords (then Rome, prospectively modern China). Fanciful on the face of it, projection of structurally induced trends across aeons of time is actually no more far-fetched than the perpetuation of an alliance into a configuration altered overnight. In fact, expanding NATO marginally too soon on the assumption of the (resurgent Russia) Macedon scenario may well set the stage for having to extend the alliance still farther eastward, and then much too late, to include Russia in order to preclude the Roman scenario. In terms of this, a China that had disposed of its Japanese (or U.S.-Japanese) Carthage in the Pacific has become ready to move westward just as Rome, triumphant in the western Mediterranean, had moved eastward.

Instead of tampering with an obsolescent military alliance, the preeminent challenge is to preclude untoward political alignments among the three Eurasian core powers. For the United States, as the preeminent Western power and profitably disinterested co-guarantor in both Euro-Atlantic and Asian-Pacific structures, this means first of all avoiding particular trends or situations rather than promoting any in particular. American statecraft should undertake nothing that directly propels or indirectly eases China into succeeding Czarist Russia as the regional, and into immediately following Soviet Russia as the globally expansive continental, challenger of the presently still dominant insular if culturally no longer predominantly Anglo-Saxon power. At the heart of Britain's pre-World War I error was accommodating the French and Russian ex-enemies rather than conciliating the only supposedly irreconcilable German antagonist-to-be. Accordingly, the United States certainly should not provocatively team up on a still grander scale with its Russian ex-enemy (as it lately did with the German ex-enemy) against a China it prematurely targets as an adversary. Nor must American policymakers do the opposite and countenance, let alone build up and play off against Russia, an economically or also more dangerously ascendant China (let alone a safely reunited allied Germany) as it also did during the Cold War. Pushing Russia into a lastingly untenable position in the Eurasian triangle will incite any Russian regime to press for a realignment. Short of the worst-case scenario of a directly West-threatening Russo-Chinese entente, a Russo-German rapprochement risks then having materialized sufficiently late in a correspondingly rigid form to be correctly construed by China's regime of any kind and disposition as anti-Chinese.

Projections from past to future structures and trends make sense when the situations and relative capabilities of the main actors and the consequent systemwide agendas are comparable. Such projections sharpen, and the hypothetical predictions they produce encourage, strategic thought, albeit of the mainly negative kind. Projections are insufficient when significant transformations in either actors, arena, or agenda make prediction based on projection less appropriate and useful than prescription implied in prophecy, propelling emphasis from negative strategy (what to avoid) toward positive strategy (how to proceed). Thought experiments that link strategy to structure are simultaneously enhanced into speculative explorations of ways to relate portents to promise.

As long as the prime thrust of grand strategy is negative—avoidance of mistakes so as to avert a hostile bid for global mastery—is there a worthwhile role for high foreign politics? Conversely, has not foreign policy been rightly reduced to strategically neutral, if not neutered, conference diplomacy and diplomatic summitry? Such diplomacy may strike one as just as sufficient among formally independent but strategically unengaged global powers, as a combination of economic and administrative, in their sum quasi-municipal, low politics is among regionally integrated polities. The correct answer is yes to the first and no to the second query at a time when the traditional rules and routines of high foreign politics are (temporarily?) relegated from spectacular maneuvers in overt crises to near-subliminal mind-sets, kept alive for hypothetical (and presumably unlikely?) contingencies.

Even reduced to its present state, high foreign politics retains three main functions. It is more than ever necessary to dam the chaos-prone dynamism of primitive, prestatist pluralism. It alone can inject a still requisite movement into the stagnation-prone geostrategic statics of poststatist communitarian pluralism. Last but not least, it alone inhibits international politics from following domestic politics into the status of devalued handmaiden of societally favored consumerism. In the latter role in particular high foreign politics substantiates the ideal attributes of statism as a set of norms as well as functions. Such politics reserves for grand strategy the normative dimension liberalism has striven to monopolize for reformist international law and organization's mission to obliterate real politics. Construing the idealistic dimension of political realism in this manner does not imply disowning the real significance of the material factor when implemented conservatively within the bounds of practical domestic politics. However, it does challenge liberalism's penchant for the low—chiefly economic and domestic—politics of socioeconomic development as the only motor behind positive evolution.

What has been said so far—or the way it has been said—points to a new shape of the perennial dialectic engaging the realist with the idealist facets of politics. However, the attribution of an ideal, including ethical, quality to the state as a value—and through it to high foreign politics as a process—cannot be extended unaltered to a mass phenomenon such as population migrations. Ancient in kind, such migrations are more than ever impervious to the diplomatic-strategic rationality and military-strategic theology residually surviving within the Eurasian issue. They are also immediately intractable by the kind of accelerated diffusion of economic prosperity that took place in much of the Asian and some of the Latin-American sector of the ex-Third

World. Uncertain how to react to such impediments, the Northern haves waver between dignifying a receptivity to invasions by the Southern have-nots that has been based on crude materialism with the pretense of world-wise pragmatism, and evading the many unresolved dilemmas into an entire-world-embracing moralism, in a perfect match with the lagging Southern have-nots' endeavor to compensate for material deficiencies by clothing them in the accoutrements of a culturally or religio-politically accented exalted idealism.

Transcending existential intricacies and ambiguities in either a well-intentioned utopia or a misdirected nostalgia cannot but impede a process aimed at resolving inescapable operational and ethical quandaries. Only a political culture that has been revised on both sides of the steadily shifting frontline between the insecurely prosperous and the rebelliously poor can initiate the perforce ingrate task of practical crisis management. With this end in view, efforts to alleviate the festering global civil-to-class conflict point decreasingly to melioristic designs-implementing nurture and increasingly to self-correcting nature working through basic political instincts and the law-like tendencies these instincts actuate.

Opposing morally self-satisfied utopianism with a species of naturalism is ethically all the more exacting for such naturalism being on the face of it even more indifferent morally than statism. Nevertheless, a realism that substitutes naturalism for the peculiar form of idealism that is at a premium in statecraft has obvious strategic and some even though less apparent normative merits in relation to the peculiarities of siegecraft, wherein the priority of each side is to outlast an unwittingly shared adversity rather than overwhelm a differently long-suffering adversary. The sturdy ethics of a return to nature negates the material and psychological assumptions behind designs intended to raise societal arrangements and social conventions high above the human condition. Such overambitious efforts engender perverse side effects in multilateral humanitarianism internationally no less than in progressivist welfare statism internally—and there only less devastatingly than in "real" when ostensibly brought down to earth from "utopian" socialism.

A politics that reemphasizes nature over nurture and shifts emphasis between statecraft and siegecraft in the two diverse arenas of world politics will avoid reactivating the "worst" features of traditional realpolitik while allowing for even presently remote or unlikely contingencies in the principal arena (e.g., China's unbridled military expansionism). A range of options is thus opened between actually applying traditional balance of power geopolitics and merely cultivating a geopolitical mind-set sensitive to the need for history's creative projection into the future. The immediate purpose, to moderate the overt application of the traditional principles and instruments among the major powers and constrain chaotic lesser-actor pluralism, can then be extended to sublimating the assumptions and aspirations behind the principles and instruments of realpolitik in relations among civilizations.

Beyond these essentially negative strategic precepts, the prophecy-related prescriptions suggest something more positive. As both a global and a regional power, the United States has a vital stake in a strategy that allows the cycles of local de- and restabilization to implement the self-correcting mechanism innate in nature. Allowing the mechanism a considerable latitude is the presently superior alternative to nurture-implementing attempts to manage the surface of local instabilities. Thus inspired interventions, committed to freezing or restoring a status quo, are static in their societal purpose or consequences and tend to be dehumanizing in their ultimate effects on people. Devolutionary implications of a disengagement that compels local adaptations are comparatively dynamic. Moreover, they tend to be ethically bracing for the disengaging polity when they compel the moral qualms caused by material self-containment to seek a counterpart in ethically revitalizing reassertion of its worth against attempts at delegitimization from within or without.

A reevaluated reality and rethought philosophy help integrate the negative with the positive facets of strategy. They disclose the manifest comparative advantage of an elastic over a provocatively static defense of Western civilization. Drawing on both assets decides the fundamental choice in favor of calculable risks incurred presently by inaction, and thus against allowing risks concealed in hyperactivity to expand into unpredictable and perhaps unmanageable dangers down the road. Addressing the linked issues that force this choice squarely and fairly is the object of a global contract yet to be drafted so as to restore politics rather than end history before consummating its arcane thrust, and to elude alien cultures while reconciling complementary civilizations, because the contract has been conceived so as to shape an uncertain future rather than allow policy to continue impotently reflecting a puzzling present.

The core purpose of the conservative revolution has been to call the citizen back to individual responsibility by reducing the state to the position of last-resort guarantor of a socially acceptable survival minimum, with a view to resituating society in a field of basic values that transcend materiality so that political stability might underpin economic prosperity. The external corollary of such a revolution is a foreign policy that offers a credible guarantee of last resort against irreversible global calamity. However, just as curtailing the welfare state is not tantamount to restoring the night watchman state, so retrenching from zealous activism is not the same as reactivating self-isolating absenteeism from the world's turmoils. A policy that would no longer automatically ensure full provision of sustenance for its negligent or feckless members at home in order to temper the associated social pathologies, is no more validly called upon to assume external responsibilities at a comparably debilitating cost to the intended beneficiaries but actual victims—different though the resulting pathology may be in the domestic core and in the periphery. America need not feel itself thus obligated for a whole range of reasons. It cannot perform correspondingly in terms of internal resource potential. It need not do so by virtue of a historically legitimated as well as potentially self-renovating sociorevolutionary precept. Finally, it is not really forced to act in this manner by any of the functional revolutions alleged to supplant all traditions in favor of undefined and presently undefinable postmodernity.

Generalized reluctance to face problematically revolutionary reality with a genuinely conservative philosophy is contrary to both the premises and the precepts of a valid new American contract with the world. This contrariness may well stifle the momentum toward a moderately social Darwinian conservative restoration even before revolution has gotten sufficiently under way to prepare the ground for eventual restoration. The foreign policy implications of the ensuing challenge can be conveyed in a set of questions, fraught with prescriptions and an even more implicit promise.

What long-term effect will have adjudicated the rights and wrongs of the immediate future-determining Theodore Rooseveltian-Wilsonian interference with the historically proven beneficial rhythms of a matured core-Western (i.e., European) state system at the beginning of the latest chain of wars? Will this effect, if retrospectively shown to be insufficiently beneficial, prove to have been sufficiently corrected by American statecraft re-creating during the Cold War some basic elements of that system's interrupted and misdirected progressive globalization? Or will an again if differently improvident activism consummate the initial failing and set back the order-formative achievement by precluding a global order's self-sustaining crystallization, unwittingly initiated by the conflict's enactment and left uncompleted by its precipitate termination?

Were a developmental arrest or, worse, backsliding to come to pass, might this not be brought about by the victor's compulsion to relive—and remake a senescent political culture through reenacting—the role and status of its maturity? Such a bid will stake everything on the actual end of not only the successfully terminated conflict but also a destructively creative history, an end deemed desirable for all even when resisted by many.

Finally, directly future-related specific questions arise from this context in the present trough between peaks of challenge and response. Will and should the United States seek, under a reformulated but essentially unaltered economic doctrine and policy, an apparently safe refuge from the burdens of real- and cultural-political dilemmas that leadership highlights rather than creates? Can such a relief be legitimately sought and will it be actually found in the proposition that the business of America is business? Surrendering the heroics constitutive of a certain kind of history (deemed obnoxious) to still vibrant civilizations and cultures means refusing compliance with the imperatives of the political side of nature (declared obsolete) in both statecraft and siegecraft.

Following the eclipse of naive religiosity, Western civilization began to be unhinged by the insufficiency of first rationalism and subsequently romanticism to provide a mundane substitute. The rush of salvationist social ideologies into the normative vacuum coincided with the entry into world politics of a polity intent on substituting the private ethics of the citizen for the sterner morality of the city, and instantly world-improving panaceas for the immemorial ways of power. Now that the secular ideologies have run their sterile course through a series of self-defeating revolutions, the need is not for yet another pretense to revolutionary change under the auspices of a particular brand of conservatism, but for a genuinely conservative restoration. The balance of America's twentieth-century merits and demerits is conjointly being brought into perspective by the conditions of the century's end, suited less for one more lurch toward world community than for a plodding advance toward a new system of order based on individual responsibility. To be both viable and genuinely progressive, this order will have to be capable of coordinating compromised unitary state-type polities with reascendent pluralistic community-type polities in a workable synthesis of history's cyclically alternating interstatist systems and empire- or community-type pluralisms. If this means a partial reversion to the austerities and disciplines of the end of nineteenth-century social Darwinism nationally, and to the rules and restraints of a concert of powers internationally, the price is acceptable so long as a superior viable alternative is imperceptible.

Actually, the cost will not prove to have been too high if the conservative restoration relights the lamps that seemed to have gone out forever in the summer of 1914, and if the guns of August are spiked not only in Europe but also in many other places. Restoration of traditional international politics is subject to modification by intervening socioeconomic and moral-political evolution. This qualification promises Europe a benign revisitation of its history, leading to the final healing of inherited divisions. It does not, however, guarantee this attenuation any more than it spares the wider West exposure to the possibility of retrogression in its place among civilizations and cultures.

From Present to Future 87

Forward-moving dialectic among ostensible opposites mediates evolution through modes of destruction that either entail reformation or compel reconstruction. Contemporary return-cum-moderation will materialize in full when earlier calamities have been finally purged. One such calamity for the West has until recently been Europe's vulnerability to a type of politics and political culture echoing early medieval addiction to passional creeds and hierarchical structures. It was, not quite accidentally, reserved for Nazism to reincarnate this atavism in a form that the already far-advanced anachronism of the earlier modes could not but corrupt further. This vitiation notwithstanding, the daemonic thrust of remobilized Germanic tribes implemented instructively the refusal of history to allow any of its integral constituents to vanish from the undercurrents of change without conclusive proof that it has been terminally exhausted. No less revealing is the contrast between the hidden gravity of this particular drama and the voluble theatricality of the Latin branch of fascism's self-identification with a Renaissance-type of realism and rationalism that had been absorbed into history more safely and surely than creedal medievalism. Invoking history without the will or power to bring it closer to consummation across Europe's full arc to begin with has little more to teach us about politics than the chiliastic utopianism of self-confessedly end-of-history communism—or the arrogant pragmatism of free-market capitalism stripped terminally of classic statism.

In the real world, Nazism's defeat opened the way to a reenactment of traditional international politics between two problematically European powers: one wholly unexposed to the medieval experience and the other largely removed from it. This reenactment's lack of authenticity has corresponded exactly to the superpowers' questionable identity. A more authentic restoration of tradition in international relations is now the necessary precursor to reaffirming in all of Europe the more benignly creedal side of medievalism, albeit one tainted by the new materiality, associated with institutionalized pluralism. In the world outside Europe, residues of earlier history move into the present and toward the future through cracks in the unfrozen crust, or only provisionally settled layers, of preexisting order. Whether this means a return to the precolonial layer in Africa or the pre-Columbian layer in Latin America, reversion exposes locally fragile modernity to the siege by a past that is as questionable as the siege's unpredictably fluctuating consequences. In Asia by contrast, this return to the past means a vastly more clear-cut and speedy race between two equally potent forces and influences: atavisms representing traditional identity and cultural authenticity, and modern materiality equipping identity and authority with enforceable potency.

Coincidentally, atavisms qua dark sides of (human) nature and particular culture can be either appeased or absorbed, albeit differently and with different prospects of success in the several areas. Residues of the past can be appeased by a statecraft that employs historically informed strategic rationality; or be absorbed by means of submersion in materiality, as part of an only postulated process of a short- or long-term imbrication of liberal economic with democratic political evolution. Superior statecraft distinguishes between the short and the long term in relations between major powers; positive submersion is fatally inhibited by medium-term evolutionary bottlenecks due to asymmetrically growing population and productivity in the least "civilized" areas. In the pervasive interlock between history and civilization, progression toward ever larger and more inclusive (regional or civilizational) polities is subject to the atavisms' eventual purgation. Positive progression will meanwhile run into inhibitions reflective of the dialectical character of evolution and amenable only to a statecraft that is sympathetic to a self-correcting political nature. This nature's subjective, essentially instinctual, side consists of progressively rationalized—rather than always rationally self-interested—responses to the dynamics and dilemmas of politics, which constitute nature's objective side galvanized by ostensibly artificial (i.e., self-created functional, technological, and institutional) innovations.

The extent or intensity of the evolutionary set-back is determined by two kinds of derangements. One takes place when the next-larger area, predesigned by criteria of economic utility, is incapable of being consolidated by means of either association or allegiance. The mere prospect of the enlargement's potential benefits will meanwhile have contributed to enhancing the perceived deficiencies of the smaller antecedent compass that had fostered the move toward a wider horizon to begin with. Such is the untoward relationship between communitarian regional union and the nation-state when it fosters ethnic separatisms in Europe, and between (post)colonial regionalism and the tribal system in Africa and its equivalents elsewhere when they succumb to chaotic pluralism. The other derangement occurs when parties, elements, or segments that legitimately belong to the larger area or entity are arbitrarily kept out of it. Such exclusion has affected eastern parts of Europe, including Russia, in relation to Europe as the larger whole, and the nondominant ethnic tribes in relation to the "nation"-state in Africa. The implied tendency will be for the excluded (and, in terms of the more inclusive values, delegitimized) entity to either coalesce in revolt or decompose into still smaller fragments. The excluding larger entity is disabled in material terms by the consequent failure to convert a more comprehensive values system into correspondingly enhanced power.

The end of history will appear on the horizon only when purging retrogressive atavisms in ever larger entities or polities is about to culminate in a fusion of global economy with world community. A particular civilization is by contrast in dire danger of passing its zenith when it has expelled statelike polity (as the particular interests transcending norm behind moral-political unity) from civil society (as the locus of utilitarian pluralism and materiality). This separation is currently far advanced in the narrow West and is characteristic of America; it can best be healed in a widespread reconciliation of the societal and statist constituents of a complete polity in a developmentally matured and expanded body politic coincident with a civilization. As a form of polity fit to receive the spirit that has been leaking out of the state pari passu with the ascent of society to economic prosperity, that civilization will survive which has coalesced economic utility with sociopolitical community and creedal allegiance within all-encompassing solidarity. History can meanwhile continue to evolve and be ever more closely entangled with civilization, not necessarily directly or deliberately but also paradoxically. It is paradoxical to affirm the positive role of ideal statism in relation to American societal pluralism for no more enduring reason than to mediate an effective transition from the nation-state to a culturally plural civilization, regarded as the henceforth primordial site of values coalesced in spirit and only comprising utility. For America to choose concurrently to identify with a broadly defined Western rather than narrowly Atlantic civilization entails, again somewhat paradoxically, a foreign policy posture reminiscent of Britain's onetime splendid isolation.

Any process or policy tending to supplant the state by civilization as the locus of ideality and allegiance will inevitably raise interconnected questions about the relation between the state and war on the one hand and between individual civilizations and the nature of their coexistence on the other. In large parts of the West, the state has been divested of spirit when the link between the state's ideal role-and-status attributes and the material assets and acquisitions supportive of civil society, implemented by war, has been severed in fact or perception. A complexly multinational world economy works—or is presumed—to disconnect the henceforth unnecessary state mystique (as distinct from state machinery) from a really or apparently self-sufficient civil society. The two interlocked disconnections are—or are supposed to be—consummated by the divorcement between contemporary polity and war. This particular rupture raises the issue of cause and effect. Does war disappear with the desacralization of the state (because it was a matter of inane prestige or a sport of kings), or is the state despiritualized as a result of the dematerialization of war (as no longer necessary for satisfying society's defining needs and greed)? When spirit is being expelled from the state, it seeks an alternative site or location to avoid being forced out of history as a secular process imbued with a meaning to be revealed at its end. The price of spirit's expulsion would be its wholesale replacement by unrestrained and uninspired lowest-grade power. As an expression of history's refusal to end prematurely and man's refusal to live without faith or outside history, spirit can migrate instead to a polity with a compass that corresponds to evolving (and only including pragmatic-economic) realities. In such a case, another question arises: what replaces war as the spiritualizing cause or attribute of the state and relations among states in interactions among regional communities or civilizations?

The replacement must be located where the connection between state and war has radically weakened if not disappeared: within the relationship between formal status projected into role and material resource. A well-functioning world economy, serving as a framework of and inducement to foreign politics attuned to the prosperity of individuals rather than the power of a supra-personal entity, will ensure sufficient resources for all main participants in the intercivilizational dialectic. The consequently created gap is not material but normative and is, therefore, not of the kind that was previously narrowed by the close link between the material well-being of a society and its concern with the status and role—or prestige and power—of the state. The striving for congruence between pragmatic utility and emotionally satisfying scope and contents of polity continues none the less. The quest is, however, substantially demilitarized when, freed from the stressfully direct connection between role and resource (productive of formalized violence) on the corporate level, it simultaneously suffers from distractions implicit in material self-seeking (for prosperity or its never sufficiently satisfying social product) individually. In these conditions, normative fulfillment can be sensibly sought and may be found within the framework of regional-civilizational commonality that is capable of expressing national identity or achieving a different form of ethnocultural subjectivity without resorting to war in its capacity as the foremost pathway or inducement to either national unity or a nation-state's disruption.

Before anything like this can transpire, the bicephalous Euro-American West must undergo a newly intense interplay with the other major civilizations. If it is to confront the test with confidence, it must at the close of the twentieth (or "American") century face up to a preliminary task. It must start reconciling the strains between continental European and insular Anglo-American principles and polities which, originating in the seventeenth Atlantic century, are inhibiting a concerted approach to the twenty first (Asian-Pacific?) century.

The sociopolitical and economic backgrounds are made up of an end-of-nineteenth-century Bismarckian attempt at a synthesis of cultural-political conservatism with socioeconomic paternalism, academically rationalized on the Continent in concepts such as cathedra socialism and pragmatically echoed in Disraeli's species of conservatism. These elements of compromise were prematurely exposed to a growth-stunting polarization between extremes: on one side ruthlessly naturalist social Darwinism, exemplified by the Anglo-American type of primitive capitalism, on the other side radically reformist social democracy culminating in the Marxian-Leninist type of revolutionary socialism. The not only ensuing, but also partly consequent, Euro-Anglo/American divergence was narrowed only in shared disaster when the socialist challenge, driving the defense of embattled capitalism's infantile imperfections toward right-wing extremism in Europe, coincided with U.S.-led economic collapse of American-type capitalism in the Great Depression.

On the more conspicuous grand strategic forefront, the critical one hundred years began with the collapse of the Bismarckian policy of German-Russian accommodation as the pillar of European order, subject to British concurrence but insulated from Britain's self-interested interference. The century took a wrong turn when the near simultaneous demise of Lord Salisbury's "splendid isolation" in Europe for the sake of freeing Britain's hands in Asia gave birth to a diplomacy of anti-German suspicions in both Europe and Asia, setting the stage for the insertion of American power and policy into a global free-for-all. The present marks the ending, or only suspension, of the ensuing negative developments on both the societal and the strategic planes in an environment altered by successive revolutions of all kinds. This peripeteia permits the resumption of an interrupted evolution on behalf of a conservative restoration that looks back to the final decade of the nineteenth century for its guidelines.

Central to Europe is once more German-Russian entente. Its indispensable facilitator and complement is again the offshore insular Anglo-Saxon power's progressive strategic disengagement from the European continent for the sake of a prompt and timely reengagement in Asia. The reasons for this reorientation are not exhausted by the causes of a parallel migration of America's internal center of gravity from the Atlantic to the Pacific rim. Economic issues are involved in Asia with a more traditional statist (as distinct from the West European communitarian) framework, a fact that suffices to upgrade the global security equation closer to the traditional plane of conservative realpolitik internationally, if only gradually and over time. As of now, this consequence links up already within the requisites of a truly grand strategy with America's domestic crisis. The economic costs of the welfare state (and its regulatory components and incidentals) that were sustainable in concert with the West European analogues against the inferior potential of the rival utopia of Eastern socialism, have to be reduced in the face of a tougher competition from the incompletely free-market techniques of Pacific zone capitalism.

A considered restoration strategy is concerned firstly with avoiding errors intervening between past and present, and only secondly with prosecuting a positive transformation of the present into a broadly envisaged future. A safe takeoff consists presently of recognizing the century between the 1890s and 1990s as one belonging to the category of more turbulent than fundamentally creative centuries—as one, consequently, in which the accomplishments do not warrant attempts at a linear projection forward. This century's first half spawned a profligate multiplicity of change-promoting innovations. Its second half has been spent in combining ostensibly rival but essentially equally unrealistic social-political experimentations with the simulation of a real political contest—a contest around the fictitious stake as to who will realize and exploit the earlier social and technological innovations to the exclusion of not only the rival other but preferably all others.

It is, therefore, not surprising that the century is ending in frustration, expressed in the poverty if not absence of original intellectual and social invention. History, though far from ending, seems to be close to having exhibited the full range of basic human and societal possibilities. This fact, which testifies to the disparity between thought and technology and to the difference between declaring and consummating revolutions, is strikingly evidenced in the ever expanding range of inconclusively stalemated *post-* and *neo*-phenomena and philosophies. *Neo-* medievalism is confined to pluralist structure without a unifying spirit capable of superseding the original's perversion in Germany's national socialism. *Neo*-isolationism is either a term of abuse from the internationalist side of the spectrum or a policy without either positive or workable definition on the would-be patriotic side. Proponents of *post*-industrial *post*-modernity search in vain for originally novel intellectual formulations of immemorial dilemmas, to serve as a basis for an actually new foundation of politics. Moreover, as the most revealing part of the vain search, the dissolution of a once comprehensible dichotomy between liberalism and conservatism has given way to the entanglement of (economic) *neo*-liberalism with (social and political) *neo*-conservatism. In the prevailing atmosphere, each strand can be passed off with impunity for the era's authentic conservatism, called to renew society even as it restores traditional culture at home without doing much that is either new or traditional about politics abroad.

Interrogation IV.
A Civilization:
Atlanticist or Euro-American?

When we look beyond the Bosnias and Rwandas, the Algerias and Haitis, we pierce to the only clumsily concealed Western fears of escalating migrations and infiltrations. What are, first, the implications of this phenomenon for world politics generally and, second, the immediate or particular consequences for the two, American and European, wings of the West?

Fundamental to the assessment of possibilities and necessities is the temporal factor. Its one part expresses a historical accident more than the achievement of policy, when it extends the time-span prospectively available for preferring masterful inactivity to rudderless muddling-through, a ranking of alternatives once favored more emphatically than practiced by another imperial and insular power. Its other part is the basic fact of contemporary politics and an integral by-product of history, consisting of the wide discrepancies in the stages of unequally Western-type evolution in different parts of the world. Awareness of these discontinuities is crucial in a setting of widely proclaimed differences in civilization- and culture-related conditions, because uneven evolution rules out with uniform rules of conduct also uniform sanctions and remedies against misconduct defined as contravention of ecumenically valid progress.

A degree of ethical relativism reflects by contrast the historicity of existential phenomena. A historically rationalized measure of relativism is justified on moral grounds and is necessitated by political considerations if Western humanitarianism is to be immune to the charge of just another, moralistic kind of cultural imperialism.

The end of a taxing interstate conflict has inevitably—and on balance desirably—inverted priorities from external or international to internal or domestic challenges and problems. This momentary inversion corresponds to a secular trend from external to internal functions of government in generating the material and ideal goods that warrant a regime's authority and confer legitimacy on a political order. Attendant on the trend is the growing ascendancy of the organic over the operational factor—of the makeup of polity over manipulation by policy—in shaping relations and determining outcomes. Concurrently relaxing external pressures and constraints on policies and promoting some kind of pluralism against statism is potentially beneficial in societies ready for community. However, this same trend will be expressed disruptively in the chaotic kind of pluralism wherein the advantage of nature over nurture, which the trend implies, is bereft of the positive value-institutional components that increasingly complement the physical and material ones as a social organism evolves and matures.

Most recently, all of the components of the organic factor have finally prevailed over the initially dominant strategic operations in deciding the outcome of a global conflict that implemented the combination of the land-sea power (or continental-maritime) schism with the East-West schism. Both of these schisms, just as the variously manifest secular-spiritual one, actualize overlapping identities rather than polar opposites despite their being rooted in discrete natural givens: land and water, the location of the sun's rise and setting, and body and soul. Lately a radical slowing down of operations among major powers has shifted emphasis from the geostrategic to the sociocultural component of the centuries-long interlock between the two schisms in Eurocentric world affairs. This unraveling has reinforced further the significance of the organic, both material and value-institutional, attributes of the (parties to the) East-West schism over the operational factor.

It is in this predominantly organismic setting that America, besieged by migrants within the Western Hemisphere as a regional power and experiencing generalized turbulence as a world power, is challenged in its national and cultural identity as a polity. This same challenge confronts Europe when refugees from its Mediterranean south exceed by far the displacements of the culturally more germane and potentially compensating escapees from post-communist East. The difference is that whereas the United States can find some relief in an isolationist correction of indiscriminate internationalism, Europe's sole recourse is in an activist correction of a de facto disengagement from self-dependent high policy sufficient to reactivate the power and the will that still persist in America and permit the latter's temporary retrenchment to mutual advantage.

Europe's historic mode of continuous evolution on an interstate basis had been disrupted through an untimely American intervention before a later U.S. engagement could foster the parent continent's pluralist-communitarian reconstruction. This incentive having done as much good as it can do, the next advance cannot be "made in the U.S.A." but must spring as much from the intangible resources of Europe's East as from an eastward extrapolation of the material and organizational assets Western Europe has salvaged from interwar depression and wartime defeat. These tangible assets, and the cultural-political norms associated with them, can serve Europe as an essential component of a future synthesis but must not be busily advertised as the unalterably ready-to-wear model for yet another passive reception in the East. Ongoing imitation risks repeating the historically common inversion of nominal convergence into effective divergence between the two Europes and blocks the possibility of a historical first—an equitable and therefore positive integration of Europe's two unevenly developed because unequally favored halves.

The Philadelphia model of federalism was propagated for the western half of Europe at an earlier stage of the Cold War, well before a European community had started evolving in muted economic competition with the United States (and with Japan and Southeast Asia). Emergence of this little Europe has been awkwardly guided by an effort to subsume, so as to jointly shelter, the statist centralism endemic to France and the federalism historically innate to Germany under a common institutional umbrella. Opposed to the product evolving functionally by fits and starts along a Paris-Brussels-Bonn axis is a greater Europe taking shape in function of a developing Berlin-Moscow axis. Such a Europe can take shape and the strategy for it materialize with the complicity of Brussels or eventually against it; with or without the blessing of a Washington willing or unwilling to learn sufficiently from World War I and its sequelae to adjust interpretation of the national to the requirements of the systemic—or civilizational—interest. Making membership in a truly "new" Europe contingent on conformity with only Western Europe's political culture and its kind of political economy—the former in all essentials and the latter at graduated speeds—is fully at variance with reequipping Europe with the will to act for political ends. The interdependent attributes of a viable polity and policy—power and will—have been forged separately and fused intermittently at different earlier stages in the development of links between technical civilization and humane culture, between the politics and economics of war, and the state and society in peace and war. The presently missing component has been irretrievably atrophied in Western Europe. If not immediately the power, the will is latently present and can be reawakened, if anywhere, in Eastern Europe.

In remote times but not incomparable circumstances, internally unifying and externally projectable energy had to be imported into Egypt's overmature commercial delta cities from the Nile's more primitive but also more vital and more eagerly unification-seeking upstream region. Much the same was substantially true for the Piedmontese highlands (as distinct from the Florentine lowlands) in Italy and the Prussian marchland (rather than Frankfurt's parliament) in Germany. For Europe today and tomorrow, this means that prerequisites of membership related to spirit will have to rank alongside, and occasionally outrank, those limited to formal institutional structures and pragmatic economic doctrines and strategies. Meanwhile, the precepts associated with such structures and strategies have not been made more authoritative or legitimate by a narrow, if historically seminal, segment of European civilization allowing itself to become too badly in need of outside assistance and too reminiscent of the onetime thin overlay of nominal Romanitas over ethno-culturally alien barbarians. "Core Europe" is now least qualified to test and screen its eastern offshoot and more than once protective barrier before certifying the "periphery"'s authentic Europeanness.

The West will reconstitute its capability for resistance by withstanding, through a deepened trans-Atlantic but not obsoletely Atlanticist strategic coordination, the many challenges to a Euro-American cultural synthesis. Europe will become a valid partner capable of shouldering a measure of devolution in behalf of a common civilization only on the strength of inner West-East equality, guaranteed by a Russo-German partnership. Only thus will Hegel be metaphorically put back on his feet from the neo-liberal adaptation of Marx's reversal of a metaphysical brand of idealism into economic determinism; an ethical state—or statist principle—writ large regionally be sufficiently reconstituted to consummate its unfinished historic mission to uplift nascent society into one that is genuinely civil because not only consumerist but also civic-minded; and truly authoritative because more than formally legitimate governments be reborn across all of Europe. Such governments will be capable of reactivating a political framework for protection against a culturally insidious threat, so as to complement psychologically insufficient (albeit also increasingly hard-to-ensure) material sustenance. Specifically in Eastern Europe, this also means that for the governments there to become authoritative, they will have to be representative more than procedurally, because they will have ceased to be more respectful of popular appetites pointing westward than of national and regional identity and dignity directing the sights of a reborn citizenry inward.

An internal strengthening of the United States is primarily a matter of societal mores and economic momentum, conducive among other things to a new balance or a more pragmatic perception of the right balance between the tangible benefits of massive immigration, legal and illegal, and the penalties inherent in deferring indefinitely a pause necessary for genuine integration (rather than mere aggregation) of an increasingly multiethnic society. A slowing down in the rate and tempo of absorption that does not translate into swift and smooth assimilation would seem to be necessary to mend a strained social fabric and safely redefine a specifically American civilization in terms that are consistent with, but necessarily different from, its vision by the eighteenth-century founders. By contrast, Europe's next renaissance is more critically a matter of moral-political than socioeconomic and ethno-cultural regeneration. It is achievable when a foreign politics inspired by an all-European patriotism countervails the materialism centered on economic prosperity in domestic politics. In order to improve on early Cold War West European neutralism, this patriotism will have to be armed with sufficient strength of purpose to fuse the formally antithetical, and globally actually antagonistic, ideal and material sides of reality into a "politics of meaning."

At issue under this or a different label is a compound of politics and ethics in a spiritually uplifting and politically energizing religiosity vastly different from U.S. or any other style religious fundamentalism. If not found there, uplift will be sought in the wrong places of either apolitically if not antipolitically private morality or only tactically constrained materiality, across a reformist range extending from Hillary Rodham Clinton to Newt Gingrich in America and from Václav Havel to Václav Klaus in Europe's geographic but, under the circumstances, not otherwise significant center.

When triumphant materialism has been saved for good from further debasement into petty hedonism, a revised and revitalized junction of enlightened realism and pragmatic functionalism will be able to flourish in variously institutionalized communitarian pluralism or confederatively moderated statism in Europe—and realigned federalism in America. Moving in this direction should ensure the defense of the West with assistance from a Europe that has transferred onto the communal institutions of an expanding union the guiding principle vanished from its moral-politically moribund if not already defunct member states. A reformulated and upgraded "reason of state" has already begun to be clamored for by the more enlightened among the Brussels bureaucrats. This austere principle of classic statecraft will, however, begin to take on life again only when a renascent Europe has empowered its developmentally retarded, but thereby also preserved, eastern half to impress upon the old continent the commitment to an enlarged *patria*, historically reserved for sociocultural and territorial marginals vis-à-vis an entity prepared or compelled to accept them on equal terms.

In America, a stance of calibrated disengagement calls for the highest form of statesmanship when statecraft along the West-East spectrum overlaps with siegecraft on the North-South axis—when, therefore, a civilization's survival makes demands on foreign policy that project a particular facet of politics' authentically tragic quality, peculiar to siegecraft, to the fore. The implied obligation is to weigh the requisites of defense of one, transcendent and abstract, positive value, pertaining to a civilization's cultural identity, against another positive value, attaching to the mitigation of conventionally "tragic" human miseries. Unlike what could be attempted in the past among great powers through an ultimately self-defeating endeavor to evade the contradiction between the imperative of self-help and the prohibition of inordinate self-assertion to guarantee the state's autonomy, no one's successful bid for a unifying hegemony can provide escape from this particular dilemma. Therefore, a more-than-ordinary tension between the (power- and interest-focused) existential givens and the normative (cultures and civilizations co-shaping) desiderata will continue to permeate all contemporary politics. By continuing, this tension will keep alive the immemorial schism between changing forms and incumbents of the spiritual and the secular principles. This tension is especially trying for a society such as the American that has thanks to a naturally favored situation been historically untouched by any but the most conventional if not commonplace kinds, features, and understandings of tragedy—better described as mere calamity.

As a result, the interpretation of the American national interest has reflected the cyclical variations between liberal and conservative expressions of a well-defined ideological dichotomy. Until yesterday, U.S. foreign policy could afford these variations with considerable impunity because a compensating degree of continuity in basic policy rested on the exceptional clarity of the structural determinant of strategy, inherent in bipolarity. This facility has departed together with the clarity of the liberal-conservative ideological dichotomy because, in all circumstances except one, national interest is not an original given but only a derivate from the makeup of the environment and the role a polity is prepared to play in it. A reevaluation of the environment and of the resulting means-ends equation had, therefore, to be addressed in these pages as the necessary prerequisite to considering specific strategies and tactics for upholding America's "national interest"—this addictive religion of overzealous converts to political realism, lifted out of the context of the concept's original formulation and the principle's enduring validity in opposition to (presently reascendant?) legalism and moralism.

To continue being valid, a great nation's interests must henceforth be defined and pursued in ways compatible with the more general—and for comparatively stable societies selfish—interest in first preserving and then expanding a modicum of global stability. Moreover, the constitution of a general order must be construed and the order be pursued in a special way: as first and foremost the prerequisite to defending a civilization that, beleaguered on the plane of culture, courts exposure to a still more portentous siege on a plane where the preservation of corporate identity is in the last resort a matter of common power.

Conclusion.
Historicist Intuition versus Postmodern Revolutions

The technological revolutions associated with new "waves" and "highways" have not generated radically novel international obligations or effective new means for meeting the commitments. Nor have they so far generated societally reforming processes or socially indisputably valuable, let alone indispensable, products. Before they terminally stultify the making of postmodern policies, the techniques had better not block the rediscovery of the intuitive tenets of immemorial statecraft. When those tenets reemerge from the lately accumulating layers of obscurity, the question marks that their proponents have prudently appended to the prophecies concerning history and civilizations[8] will be reassuringly answered negatively by the positive restoration of politics.

Advancing technologies empower societies and polities to the advantage of individuals who, able to acquire and master the new knowledge, can use it in support of their economic interests and aggregate economic growth. Simultaneously, the proportion of a gross national product devoted to either national military defense or available for politically sustainable economic expenditure abroad can decline even when strategy is fixated inertially on military preparedness and reoriented progressively to readiness for low-cost humanitarian assistance. However, the new technology will do more harm than good when it obstructs an alternative perspective that depends much less on information than on intuition and less on the new kinds of knowledge than on historically and normatively shaped understanding. If this is a paradox, consistency obtains when the preservation and correct redirection of the principal intellectual resources infringe on the otherwise unchecked growth of the monopoly of a mere skill (formal diplomatic) in the making of foreign policy—an equivalent on the intellectual and elite level of the devalued old-fashioned manufacturing skills on the material and mass levels.

Foreign politics will be fully restored to its traditional connection with intuitive understanding when technological revolutions have spread political culture without further demeaning the contents of wider culture, and updated the techno-organizational facet of civilization that affects collective power without downgrading the sociobehavioral facet that reflects and shapes individual mores. When technology has proven itself capable of such creativity, innovations will extend rather than terminate the time-span available to history while civilizing its course. Propelling history past negative portents toward any worthwhile promise will continue to be the task of a conservative statecraft that can renew forgotten aspects of politics without pretending that the innovation is revolutionary, because it did not abjure tradition so that actually restored politics might appear to be new. Such a statecraft and such politics will emerge from the refusal to equate defusing the geopolitically shaped perils of territoriality with unconditionally surrendering to economically driven transnationality—that is to say, when statecraft has not sacrificed the charisma of the ethical state, or its enlarged communal successor, to the chimera of civil society's readiness to extend bureaucratic rationality and material utilities beyond its internally eroding and externally beleaguered Western core.

Like everything else, the relationship between society and the state, crucial for defining a civilization in its capacity as power, is at its most problematic in and for a hegemonic polity, such as the United States, located by virtue of its status squarely at the intersection of two critical relations: of the salient polity to the global environment and of domestic to globally significant foreign politics. Moreover, the state versus society problem is most acute when the hegemonic polity itself approaches, bestrides, or nervously tests itself against its own actual or perceived high point. It then hesitates between revolution and reform as the seemingly complementary but covertly or openly competitive pathways to internal regeneration as the sole cure, by precisely unknowable means, for the pathology of definitive regression: regeneration in the image of a heroic or only sturdy infancy for the sake of sustainable maturity, and regression into conditions inviting unfriendly and uninvited bids for someone else's irreversible succession. It is at this point that America's efforts at updating society's economic proficiency, with assistance from reactivated individual responsibilities in domestic politics, merge with the challenge to refurbish its moral-political authority on the plane of foreign policy by reinventing itself (or, perhaps, belatedly inventing itself) as a state. This has to be done, if at all, in terms of not only basic real political integrity (by readjusting capability to claims or role to resources), but also cultural-political identity (by subsuming internal cultural heterogeneity into a more comprehensive civilizational entity).

It is questionable whether the challenge can and will be met by either of the presently dominant prescriptions alone—the would-be revolutionary retrogressive formula or a more modestly reformist progressive formula. One prescription favors a return to classic liberalism under the auspices of cultural conservatism. For the sake of liberating the forces of material wealth creation it would unleash all the resources of technological innovation, while its proponents hope to dam the societally disintegrative consequences by the policing resources of an invigorated state and the rescuable elements of traditional disciplines. The other prescription is committed to scaling down the unfulfillable promise of a societally overinvolved later, postclassic liberalism. Its proponents abjure utopianism in favor of somewhat more culturally conservative but still socially compassionate pragmatically centrist reformism. Neither the former (at present Gingrichian-congressional) nor the latter (currently Clintonian-presidential) approach to America's domestic crisis as a society has been related either comprehensively or comprehensibly to America's international dilemmas. Nor could either approach have been so related with any ease so long as crisis and dilemmas are intertwined within this country's ambiguously shaped identity, internally cleft between only inchoate, if not covert, statism and salient, but insufficient, societal pluralism. Whereas the latter has historically been isolationalist and is only potentially multilaterally institutionalist, the former has become internationalist in principle and is inevitably hegemonical in both denied ambition and actual practice.

It is easier to locate reasons for the several disconnections than to devise a correction and then implement the remedial procedure. Until recently, domestic and foreign politics were closely connected by the mutually reinforcing requirements of an externally strong state and internally stable society, under the unspoken presumption of the ultimate (arguably nondemocratic) primacy of foreign policy. The connection was forged on the narrowly societal interclass plane out of concern to outmatch the chief ideological enemy (the "socialist" system), and on the interrace cultural plane out of regard for a major ideological battleground (the "developing" world). Waging the contest effectively imposed an equal impulse toward reform for and restraint on exactions by differently disadvantaged and disaffected elements of society. The state's strategic optimum was ideally as well as practically at one with a societally indispensable minimum of equity. This near causally reciprocal determination, with an auspicious bias in favor of foreign policy needs, has in the presently emergent environment been certain to loosen to the advantage of domestic priorities. A formerly determinate relationship oscillates currently between effective segregation of the two arenas of politics and mere parallels, symmetries, or formal consistencies between them.

Segregation entails limiting government internally for socioeconomic reasons in the name of long-term solvency while maintaining governance abroad by means of a particular military instrument for the sake of immediate security. The unintended consequence is the possibility that expenditures for security will undermine expectations attached to growth in stability. A superior harmony between the two desiderata is, conversely, implicit in a symmetrical reduction of involvements in both arenas for the sake of different but complementary kinds of savings. This strategy will be driven by the desire to reinforce the domestic base so as to develop the means for reentering the international arena in force when the need for massive reinvolvement has manifestly increased. A measure of oscillation between segregation and symmetrization with respect to goals and procedures is normal in an actually or supposedly revolutionary period of transition. However, oscillation turns easily into evasion of choice between options, when negotiating the transition by carefully calibrated sequential steps becomes the victim of schizophrenic indecision. This has been the case whenever a declared (executive) disposition to lead is contradicted by the (congressionally fueled) hesitation to deliver, hiding behind arguments from either Cold War-type strategic realism or post–Cold War economism-cum-pacifism. Especially when this comes to pass conjointly with or subsequent to a burst of diplomatic or humanitarian activism, the temptation will be great to apply a well-known injunction to America's leadership pretension.

What is the price for not only reequipping that power but also reorienting its uses into correspondence with the conditions and the needs of not only the parochial but also the wider community? The price goes up when capacity for rational reform of institutions grows as a polity or civilization ascends to its climax, but the proportion of deficiencies that can be mended institutionally declines concurrently in favor of types of distress immune to organizational remedies—a class of inchoate ordeals antecedent to the deficiencies which improved organization has been able to manage at something like the midpoint of the polity's or civilization's evolution.

Contemporary America is catching up with the predicaments of modern Europe in the process of becoming a normal Western country. In doing so, it is incurring the conjunction of developmentally earliest distress with late-evolutionary distempers. It is thus overchallenged, moreover, after using up much of the institutionally realizable reformist potential of what is normally the midterm climacteric, but in the case of an infant America capable of drawing on Europe's early maturity was the originally formative period.

Nor is this all. Crisis is at its deepest when it combines the lowering effect on morale of societal decay with the state's actual or suspected decline relative to substantive assets of hypothetical (and thus all the more enervating) others. This compound of adversities has customarily invited appeals from the mundane sin of moral corruption to the salvationist promise of rediscovered and reaffirmed supernature. Impervious to this kind of remedy, modern society seeks recourse in institutional surgery inferior to prolonged societal therapy that would release the spontaneities of a polity's better nature. When problems seem or actually are insoluble because they are embedded in a generationally and otherwise lopsided socioeconomic structure, pathology may be amenable only to radical changes in a societal organism's psychology. A fundamental psychological posture from which contemporary Americans might start to mend, at the cost of much pain, is one that replaces addiction to the many past revolutions of rising expectations with the acceptance of an evolution of declining presumptions, headed by the conceit of exceptionality.

Overcoming this deeply implanted assumption and scaling down the long cherished anticipations that are attached to it is beyond the task of politics. But process can be helped along by policies: domestic programs that qualify reform with rigor so that individual or group rights are tempered by the acceptance of civic and communal obligations; and external strategies that constrain pretensions sufficiently by the requisites of performance to buttress claimed rank and asserted role with adequate resource while exposing all three "r" words to a fourth and fifth—risks sufficiently real to warrant the pretension but no greater than necessary for the performance to be strategically rational.

Implementing a newly complex equation that highlights the lost facilities of reciprocally causal connections between domestic and foreign policy will take longer than did overcoming the more clearly defined challenge. Facing up to the task means exchanging a well-deserved peace dividend for the frustrations of a global class war barely a moment after besting such a war's left-wing proponent. To complicate matters further, it means protecting an "open" society from the consequences of being opened up too widely to all kinds of abuses at home even as it must be shielded against closure by an ethno-culturally totalized version of community barely twice as many moments after defeating such a community's right-wing embodiment. Having to do all this, and do it simultaneously, would rank as a historically unprecedented injustice were it not yet another illustration of history's perverse creativity and ultimate equity. Acknowledging and addressing the problem without pretending to bring about single-handedly its solution will absolve America of the moral-political liability lurking in an especial favor of geography: the enjoyment of directly or indirectly profitable immunity to the outer world's turmoils for most of this country's history.

106 Conclusion

Projecting the present against the past is easy. Projecting it also into the future is all the more necessary for being difficult. In this dual perspective, America's predicaments have the ultimate merit of harboring the occasion for delivering an irrefutable proof that a political culture can be safely insulated from and rise above the worst of prosperity-based mass culture. For the higher kind of culture to simultaneously deepen and widen is a fit response to challenges that are more demanding than dramatic. Proving equal to them will help in answering affirmatively the question posed at the beginning of this inquiry. America's sheer being for the sake of acting on the world will have been on balance a good thing when this nation has completed the appointed time of a hegemony that was able to continue avoiding the need for coercion so long as it mediated history's natural progression.

Charting a course for such a phantom hegemony in the second instalment of contemporary America's role in world affairs, one that would midwife a "new world order" after performing this service for a rudimentary global state system, requires something else than more information from conventionally narrated history. In its place, historicist intuition relates past via the present to the future, armed mainly with imagination and aiming at history's uses in action. A thus informed intuition replaces ideology in producing an "imagined community" on a global scale, one taking shape as part of a progression that corrects the liberal postulate of linear progress with the overcoming of portents implicit in cyclical reversion. A premier world power designated by its position to mediate this kind of historical progression toward a new world order has presently to preside, armed with this particular kind of knowledge, over a triangular relationship among appropriately changing balance of power or alternate forms of equilibrium, hegemony or empire of different scope and structure, and the overall environment in the form of an interstate system or alternative framework of order. The principal change or changes conducive to sustainable order entail prospectively a movement from coercion to indirect control with respect to the hegemony/empire dimension and mandate expansion in terms of space and extension of time as against constriction of either with respect to the balance of power versus hegemony issue. As for the environment, it ideally evolves consistently with the relaxation (of control and space/time) from a constraining to a permissive structure.

Relaxing the operation of the balance of power entails expansion (globalization) and deconcentration (regionalization) in terms of space as it is envisioned by the strategist. Concurrently extended is the time perspective and, therefore, the reaction time considered necessary to address shifts in power relationships. In consequence, there is less emphasis on preemption of supremacist goals of other (normally continental) states on the part of the (insular) arbiter-balancer, apt to constitute a self-fulfilling prophecy by way of such a goal's imputation. There is by contrast more tolerance for protraction in favor of a positive presumption: that of an organic transformation of the principal assertive actor of the moment and of the both consequent and concurrent operational transformation of the total force field, apt to generate ever new or resuscitate dormant forces able and willing to counteract the threatening ascendancy of one particular actor and make up for the decline of other actors.

Within a thus restructured or just rethought spatial/temporal setting, globalization of the perceived theater permits (properly construed) appeasement of a regionally assertive great power by means of conceding it operational latitudes within limits that permit such an actor's eventual containment with the assistance of the widest range of both the existing and the actually or prospectively emergent external forces—the latter precipitated into self-affirmation by the partial disengagement of the preeminent (or phantom hegemonic) power. Russia or China are the eligible parties to be alternately or interchangeably appeased as well as contained under the supervision of the United States. Factoring in long-term trends is no small matter in circumstances that will be shaped in the next century by the consequences of the decision, wise or unwise, to accommodate China on basically its terms and rebuff the Soviet bid for a contrary sequence in the process of worldwide West-East appeasement.

As part of temporal protraction and spatial expansion of power balancing, regionalization favors conditional disengagement of the premier global power and devolution of primary regional order constitutive responsibilities to former local empires or hegemons, Germany and Russia in Europe and Japan and China or also India in Asia. A U.S.-sponsored and supervised devolution can simultaneously monitor the greater and activate the lesser regional states, propelling the latter toward performing as active agents of the integration or even (con)federalization process within areas where the informal spheres of the local great powers overlap as well as between the major states themselves. Deprived of an immediately more alluring alternative, such intermediate smaller states will assume more responsibility for themselves in order to avoid becoming the passive objects of either competitive or condominial intergreat-power strategies or arrangements. Under this hypothesis, the United States confines itself to guaranteeing both the great regional powers and the lesser states against an arbitrary preemption of the integrative process by any of the bigger players until such time as the process has taken off sufficiently to become self-sustaining.

A permanent position of balancer between rival regional powers is thus exchanged for the implicitly self-liquidating role of an integrative federalizer, reminiscent of British efforts among various kinds of its dependencies before and during the terminal decolonization process. Overall, however, this strategy of deconcentrating the balance of power/hegemony arena concurrently with its globalization differs from the traditional balancer role as practiced by Britain. Rather than deconcentrate, this kind of balancer centralized the balancing process around one suspected would-be hegemon and opposed to devolutionary regionalization of the global arena this arena's partition by means of a categorical division (between continental Europe to be stalemated and the oceanic arena to be thus opened to British monopoly). Nor was the temporal dimension extensible and the reaction time actually protracted in view of Britain's weak metropolitan base relative to the critical continental parties. Favoring precipitation of the process (via imputation of hegemonic ambitions) over its protraction (for the sake of merely supervised or also managed transformation), this particular handicap reinforced the era's prevailing general presumptions about war and peace with the result that the British perspective and actual performance were about the same in mid-eighteenth and the first half of the twentieth century: when the combined overt stake (in competition with France) was dominance in North America and preeminence in Europe, and when the hidden core issue (over and above the challenge by Germany) revolved around the rate and consequently the form of introducing a sovereign independent United States into a still Eurocentric balance of power effectively globalized by America's (and one or two Asian powers') activation.

Was this insertion to be gradual in response to intra-European and consequently global dynamics and occur conjointly with America's political maturation in peacetime? Or was it to be—as it actually became—spasmodically intermittent and then disruptively so for all parties during major wars? Presently recovering some of the lost advantages of the missed alternative entails reversing the "British" approach, implicit in centralizing the balancing process in and around NATO (against either Russia or China or a faceless hypothetical would-be supremacist) with the effect of repartitioning the European or global arena between a NATO zone of peace and stability and the rest: Russia-centered Eastern Europe and China-centered global East. Progressing instead into the future by way of a balance of power strategy that operates through expansion (appeasement of regional major powers by concession of finite latitudes within a globalized theater and extended time perspective), devolution (regional deconcentration), and substitution (of emergent for existing, including U.S., assets and agents), means implementing a trend that conforms with America's larger and safer metropolitan base than was Britain's.

After responding to pragmatic common sense, a substantial revision of strategy is vindicated by historicist intuition because it represents a modified reversion to antecedents to conventional balance of power. Moreover, it constitutes a modification of the occidental by the oriental approach to the balance of power/hegemony issue—a modification conducive to replacing clash between civilizations with intercivilizational dialectic.

Consistent and deliberate balancing of power becomes a strategy when it exceeds the operation of the raw instinct of self-preservation. Developed thus at all times and in all places, the upgraded mode reemerged in Europe in response to the restored capacity to perpetuate territorial and other acquisitions by means of effective control backed by organized coercion. The necessity to foreclose enlargements that risked becoming irreversible replaced the spontaneous rebalancing due to the propensity of inordinate empire-like power aggregations to dissolve by virtue of their inadequate capacity for internal organization sufficient to convert cumulation of assets into their integration. The contemporary or plausibly prospective functional equivalent of this propensity to dissolution is the operational primacy of organic transformations. Growing inability to control this spontaneous rise/decline dynamic by any kind of organization or counteract it by contrarily oriented strategies is conducive to accommodation rather than competition among power centers, a trend that devalues traditional balancing as a process concurrently with its stake, object, and precipitant: the attribution of the highest value to the autonomy of the primary format and framework of social existence, the state emerging from post-Roman Empire chaotic pluralism. The other values-related modifier of the balancing practice is the oriental bias in favor of relying on the cultural factor. In this tradition, an aggressor/expansionist's long term weakening (or "mellowing") is consigned to its subversion, absorption, or containment by the temporarily overwhelmed party that may be physically weaker but represents a higher civilization. This approach (summed up in the prescription to "bend with the wind") operated within the Sino-centric universe to moderate when it was not substituting for intervals of nakedly brutal and clinically pure power politics unattenuated by even the conventions and rationalizations gradually evolving in the West.

When the oriental modifier is extended from solely cultural to also pragmatic economics-related terms, it contributes to an intercivilizationally shaped evolutionary process in a way that is contrary to elementary power balancing but complementary to the modifier's role in the empire component of any prospective interregional "new world order." Contrarily to the primacy of interactor security in the multistate European system, the oriental practice supplies the emphasis on internal stability within an empire shielded by insulation from equivalent or nonrecognition of coexistent power centers (and only intermittently exposed to conventionally unmanageable intrusions).

110   Conclusion

This situation is being reproduced by the ongoing conversion to the primacy of intra- and interreginal stability over security, predicated on the assumed and largely actual immunity to frontal violent assault by a qualitatively comparable rival organism (again as distinct from difficult-to-manage but less overtly menacing alternative challenges). Whereas this change represents an increase in intercivilizational symmetry with respect to a key feature of order, continuity with respect to the issue of control is implicit in the reversion to decentralized power aggregations in post-Roman Empire early Europe.

These aggregations, too, were dependent for cohesion less on direct control by coercively enforceable means than on a special kind of indirect control mechanism. A ruler viewed as appointed and (because long-lived and male heirs-producing) manifestly approved by a still higher power passed his legitimacy on to the realm itself by a species of multi-stage normative devolution corresponding to the organization of the universe along a vertical chain of being while ensuring a necessary minimum of cohesion for the primitive body politic horizontally. The progressively institutionalized confessional principle and implement of cohesion, erected over decreasingly transcendentalist (Carolingian to Norman to Hohenstaufen) empires, within the community of Christendom has now been replaced by transnational economic ties within this community's mundane successor. So also the source of indirect control resting on the supreme hegemon's mandate to His agent on earth, while actually deriving from the original exercise of physical force, can be—and is actually being—repositioned more widely in adhesion-inducing economic factors and functions away from coercion-dependent military and other assets and instrumentalities.

A historicist insight into contemporary geopolitics supportive of convergence between civilizations mandates deconcentration of the balance of power strategy and theater. Contemporary geoeconomics allows for and facilitates decentralization of regional empire structures into informally imperial great-power spheres of interest and orbits of preponderant influence, held together by shared utilities of the major and the minor constituents provided economic interdependence is used to penalizing the former for abuses against the latter with compelling efficacy. This model of world order is sufficiently traditional in its basic principles and norms of conduct to be realistic, and is sufficiently adaptable to and sustained by the present global environment to be also progressive relative to the cruder contemporary antecedents.

In this kind of environment, the decisive influence passes from structure to strategy and the emphasis within strategy from capability qua power as an internally coherent if specifically undifferentiable "organic" entity and unmeasurable quantity to qualitatively discrete constituents of national or collective resources that are separately usable as instruments for the achievement of equally discrete purposes. As part of this disaggregation, an at least provisionally conspicuous salience of the economic over the military-political factor does more than facilitate the transition from direct to indirect control/cooperation arrangements by altering together with the quality of hegemony (from military to political) also the optimum manner of exercising the political variety. Insofar as the supremacy of economics is not only conjunctural (i.e., reflects a temporary lull between political and military crises) but is structural or even systemic, it actually modifies the core principles if not the very nature of politics. It does this by bringing into the open features of human nature previously counteracted by ideal compensations for material scarcities and their source in natural catastrophes. As hegemonism mutates into hedonism, coercive empires ascend all the way toward consensual communities by way of informal great-power orbits implemented through various forms of association. Economic growth is the principal concern of these progressivist improvements, economic assets are their principal war chest against the perils of recession, and the assets' prospective diffusion among members is the principal cement: conciliator of internal dissensions and substitute for centralized coercion.

In the process, the prevalence of the economic factor permeates increasingly all the schisms and dichotomies—statist-societal, land-sea power, and relatedly West-East and South-North, all subsumed in the existential-normative tension—that shape the arena and the agenda of world politics and affect the prospects for order. The focus on economics may historically be mercantilist, Marxist, or market-centered monetarist or other, varying mainly in the degree of political control it does actually impose upon or only implies for economic processes and societal utilities on behalf of assumed or actual state necessities. The related basic difference between continental and insular polities, affecting their kinds of empires or hegemonies and regional organizations or alliances, has incidentally opposed the short- or medium-term advantage of one-time meteoric rise/decline cycle of the insular-mercantile type of polity or hegemony to the longer and sturdier fluctuative crisis-reform-crisis trajectory of the continental variety.

This divergence can be muted with implicit advantage for the United States in conditions that allow for the contrasting practices to be combined and the different propensities to correct one another: spatially in amphibiously equipped and constituted continental-oceanic regional orders, organizations, or "common markets," all the more readily because, temporally, the slower developing continental-military polities will meanwhile have progressively acquired a sufficient capacity to realize the potentialities that had already materialized in the oceanic-mercantile alternative. Such regional compounds or hybrids may be even spared the necessity to retrace the insulars' intervening periods and conditions when the instrumental conveniences of mostly indirectly operative control mechanisms, peculiar to the combination of attraction and inhibitions exerted by economic entanglements, have been suspended by the countervailing force of ethnically motivated revulsion that deepens while nationalism awaits its extinction by materialism.

A protectionism-prone mercantilist system will encourage expansion into empires and the latter's consolidation and concentration under political and administrative controls. But it also favors their spontaneous consolidation so long as the dependent or lesser parties can not expect to survive materially on their own at levels of sustenance assured by tolerably equitable distribution of the aggregate product and allocation of the common goods. Dissolution is the ultimate consequence of discrimination when the latter has been translated into exploitation of the peripheries by the center in ways defeating viable readjustments of the authority-autonomy-stability equation. Conversely, the liberal market economy tends to dissolve traditional formal empires because they cease to be necessary for the dominant elites or polity and the dependents alike in the case of insular-mercantile empires. As for illiberal continental-military empires, they have ceased to be competitive in relation to the more liberal ones—a tendency relating the experience of the Soviet empire to that of France relative to Great Britain as well as, between continentals, Austria relative to Prussia before German unification.

This difference is apt to shape East-Central Europe as it incurs the transition from Germany's Third Empire to a fourth and from the Soviet to a second neo-Czarist Russian more or less benign replica of the sundry originals. Progressive political liberalization of continental powers and empires has historically occurred in conjunction with their relative decline in terms of material power. A more or less liberal market-type economy makes it in addition presently possible to reconstitute traditional empires on an informal basis and renounce political control in favor of pragmatic calculation of costs and benefits. The result of combining the political and the economic aspects of and reasons for liberalization is to dissolve the "mercantilistic" linkage between military (security) and economic (sustenance) facets of power, with obvious advantages for the spontaneity but potential risks for the stability of a future world order.

The invisible hand of mercantilism's opposite can cause domestic crises between the haves and the have-nots within the most advanced of national or imperial economies. But it also transfers from coercive mechanisms of empire to spontaneously operative systemic factors the capacity to differentiate the residually dependent (because nonviable) from essentially independent (because more self-reliant) lesser former members of earlier empires or alternative types of regional order. Moreover, this same invisible hand's incarnation in an anonymous "system" will redistribute the lesser parties among alternative or competing new-type informal "empires" as an expression of natural progression. This state of things is favorable to a world power willing and able to collaborate nonintrusively with nature's manifestation in history and avoid interference with such progression's traffic accidents arising out of local malfunctioning of the process or a particular political culture's maladaptation to its requisites.

As the phantom hegemon called upon to mediate progression by cooperation with nature, the United States presides willy-nilly over movement toward this prospective configuration of a "new world order." Supported by the two pillars of a revalued equilibrium mechanism and process (geostrategically amended balance of power/hegemony, expanded functionally and institutionally) and a revised empire formula (transformed from formal into informal and from coercive to unevenly consensual regional arrangements), such an order will shape and be shaped by an environment that favors functions over structure configured in terms of capabilities and institutionalization over strategic improvisations while geopolitical, economic, and ethno-cultural factors and concerns alternate in determining the comparative impact of the structural-cum-strategic and the functional-cum-institutional strands in the fabric of policies.

Thus situated, the foreign policy of America as a society and polity is strongly challenged to gravitate toward informal free-trade imperialism in response to the economics-first bias of a newly permissive and spontaneously regionalized global environment tending to pluralism. Yet the United States is also called upon to adjust a to-be-developed statist potential in tandem with high foreign politics to the revised imperatives and expanded latitudes of the balance of power in the residually constraining Eurasian sector of the environment. Relaxing the approach to the balance of power will reinforce all the givens and tendencies that have already reduced the importance because the necessity of cultivating the external strategic framework of informal free-trade imperialism, in either the British nineteenth-century manner or the more recent American fashion, in the Fourth World sector and beyond.

De-formalizing empire reduces the political and moral responsibilities habitual within the area of administrative or only managerial involvement. Spawned by mercantilism, this accountability was perpetuated in America's de facto empire that rose coincidentally with resistance to mercantilism's consummation in totalitarianism. Relinquishing an empire of this kind does not automatically translate into becoming a free-wheeling omnipresent balancer—except of the provisionally federalizing kind. Voluntary resignation from empire reduces the tendency, because it annuls the necessity, to practice intervention abroad as a rule rather than an exception. It permits enlightened self-containment because it augments the need for replenishing domestic resources and energies. Moreover, de-formalization of empire shares with relaxation of the balancing process the quality of undeniable consistency with democracy in general and the American type of democracy in particular—an attribute the role of either a flexible balancer or a steadfast manager of a merely de facto empire does not seem to possess. The license of selectivity outside the obligations accruing from a guarantee of last resort, peculiar to the role of a mere phantom hegemon and status of the preeminent world power, reflects accurately the untidy amorphousness of American democracy over and above its settled core of fundamental values and principles. Spatial expansion and temporal extension peculiar to the balance of power component allow for the clarification of issues and of the "national interest" they involve that is sufficient as well as necessary to activate a democracy's periodically suspended capacity to act on issues engaging other major powers. By the same token, informality of the empire component delegates to the momentary mood of a democratic society the decision to act or abstain from acting on disorders involving lesser polities without fatally damaging the external demonstration effect.

Thus, on both counts, strategic space is widened materially or metaphorically for either isolationist nonintervention or massively unilateral or nominally multilateral interventionism. The present mix of continuity and change and of statism and pluralism is finely matched by America's strategic commitment that is more stringent than in the pre-World War I and interwar periods and less burdensome than in the World War II and Cold War interludes. The stage is set for the experimental process of articulating and perfecting an "American way of (foreign) politics"—a synthesis of experiences with empire, balance of power, and self-isolation—to counteract the effects of the "American way of war," which replicates oscillation between isolationism and interventionism in the alternance of complete self-removal from the arena with technological overkill. Absent reciprocally stabilizing adjustments, the product of military technological revolutions in never ending succession will become the mark of America's exceptionality that waxes even as sociopolitical and cultural uniqueness wanes. It remains to be seen whether and if so to what extent this particular prowess—a triumph of America's organizational and instrumental concretism doing duty for political realism—relegates America to unwanted isolation from the rest of mankind even as involvement with its affairs unsteadily deepens. Will an aptitude that positions the United States on a different planet in terms of a conventional military technology better suited to expansive self-assertion than to intercontinental self-defense keep America sufficiently in touch with the real world to sustain leadership of this world operationally rather than subvert it morally or psychologically?

It is unlikely that, unaided by intuition, either the normative or the existential quandaries will be resolved to the advantage of either a narrowly American or the more broadly Western civilization by a military byproduct of the postmodern technological revolutions that is such a conspicuous prop in the stagecraft of American Byzantium. More will be needed if lopsidedly over- and underarmed America, no longer the western Rome-like empire that rose and fell in contention with differently incarnate Asia, is to fulfill the mandate of history. That is to say, becomes, in contrast with its initially likewise militarily proficient eastern-Roman antecedent, more and longer the lighthouse at the promontory of a civilization looking toward a new dawn than the fortress of last desperate refuge for a beleaguered civilization. This is America's inalienable choice as it faces in one or another role the alternately receding and reascending eastern counterparts across two oceans and a megacontinent that merely enlarge the challenge offered previously by mere narrows separating two lastingly inseparable mainlands.

Illuminating natural progression with historically based intuition implies adopting a systemic over against a systematic, because essentialist over against an empiricist, intellectual approach to relevance for the future as an alternative to historiographically immaculate exploration of the past for its own sake. The intuitive approach is at its highest—and is most venturesome—when it abandons induction for deduction of a special kind: i.e., from assumptions and perceptions about human nature, generative of present tendencies and harboring future probabilities in function of historically variable means for realizing an always limited range of alternative possibilities. When ostensible trends seem to favor the assumption which favors materialist over normatively idealist features, international politics tends to descend from the plane of the tragic via the farcical to the merely prosaic at a cost in nobility questionably compensated by enhanced utility. At that point, the restoration of politics must begin with its reconstruction at a low from which the only way is up toward realigning civilization with history in ways that redeem what is paltry or perverse in both.

The questions posed by the "decline and fall" of a co-imperial peace can be presently addressed only in terms unlikely to provide comfort for the romantic realist, with his peculiar brand of idealism, or satisfy the genuine conventional idealist. The present does open up, however, still-shadowy perspectives on future processes. The main immediate effect may be no greater than to temper the causal circularities that increase with the decline of pressing calamities, but without undoing all that is potentially reassuring in cyclically construed continuities. Presently most prominent circularities are those between the domestic and the global systemic, the societal and the statist, determinants conditioning foreign policies and affecting world order. They have not been made less frustrating and their product is not less arcane when the principal calamities migrate from war-prone manifestations of high foreign politics to less exaltedly lodged sociopolitical crises. Powerfully assisted by the information and knowledge revolutions, the entailed salience of economics is poised to have an indeterminate effect on international relations. This effect will be mainly negative in the medium run with respect to statecraft if assigning monopoly to economic instrumentalities overwhelms politic sensibilities in grand strategy. It can be positive in the longer run with respect to the crises that lack alternative and superior modalities for organizing an effective siegecraft. Which effect prevails over which will depend on whether historicist intuition or materialistic instinct predominates within human dispositions, this core determinant of politics objectified in the inclination of a more inclusive nature toward either reformist or revolutionary responses to the disparate ills of the two uncomfortably coexisting cities of man.

When perspectives on the future are shadowy and the present has to be reconstructed before politics can be restored, the normative environment logically becomes prior to the existential milieu. That is to say, a grand strategy must first shape the environment along an imaginative range extending beyond projection-based prediction to prophecy and beyond prescription to fantasy that, drawing on the resources of the anterior steps, completes understanding through the ascent from the empirically plausible by way of the ethically problematic to the esthetically satisfying. Only when successively rethought and reshaped can environment resume determination of routine politics. Joining the actual and the normative facets of the global milieu into an operative matrix of world politics has in the process become a matter of basic choices reflecting fundamental alternatives sustained by "objective" assumptions and "subjective" preferences.

The critical international environment consists mainly of the principal great powers and only secondarily of the less clearly crystallized remainder. The great-power core can currently mean only the United States or comprise also Germany, China, and Japan, plus Russia's relations with the United States alone or also chiefly Germany in Europe and China in Asia. In either the uni- or multipolar version of structure (and uni- or multifocal perception), the specifically great-power and generically statist level constrains behavior because it operates in terms of rules ultimately centered on the extreme possibility of one-sided or mutual coercion. Conversely, the pluralist-societal plane or sector is relatively rule-less and operates along the range from direct to indirect control, except when this "rule" is softened or obscured within the institutionalized realm of communitarian pluralism.

In both the uni- and the multipolar context, Russia can be regarded and treated in two contrasting, essentially statist or pluralist ways: as the "sick man" of Europe constituting in ethno-cultural, economic, and associated real political terms the main part of a pluralistic problem area (the ex-Soviet space) or, alternatively, as a regionally privileged and globally coequal great power in being or again becoming. In the "pluralist" perspective, the critical issue replicates the pre-World War I dilemma regarding the disposition of decaying Ottoman and Chinese empires. Its present version centers on the question whether any one great power (the United States now just as Britain or Russia before) can exercise indirect control over the whole, or the whole will be in some way partitioned and the several parts allocated more or less concertedly or competitively among several major powers (including Germany from the west and Turkey, Iran, or China from the southeast) for more direct control, preponderant economic influence or profit, and preferential geostrategic access. By contrast, in the "statist" (great-power) perspective, the corresponding alternatives are a partnership or special relationship with the United States as the foremost if not single great power (a connection certain to be highly and lastingly intolerably unequal) and diversely assorted diplomatic, economic, and even security relationships or associations with several great powers.

In the unipolar version of the pluralist problem area perspective, the United States approaches the Russian part of the problem with a strategy of informal free trade imperialism (and, rarely but massively, interventionist militarism) peculiar to an offshore insular/maritime power mixing a monopolistic ambition or agenda overseas with a pretension to the role of a continental arbiter. The aim is indirect control over the whole area and the method mixes liberal economics with rudimentary power politics in shaping the progressively redesigned strategic framework of the essentially informal approach. In the Russian context the controversial issues feature such things as the location and direction of oil pipelines in Central Asia, while incidentally providing legitimate reasons or only convenient pretexts for defensive nationalistic-imperialistic reactions on the Russian side.

From the opposite, multipolar intergreat-power, perspective the United States is and acts as the "merely" preeminent great power among a number of major states. It treats Russia as a (past, present or future; actual or potential and prospectively useful as well as legitimate) great power with appropriate regional rights and privileges. No different from America's in *its* sphere, the Russian privileges are to be exercised as much as possible by means (economic, cultural, etc.) that become comparable with America's as Russia's resources and, with them, attractiveness improve. Meanwhile, the methods ought not to be so shocking as to discredit the whole institution of regional interest spheres as one of the two principal pillars of a future world order (the other being a relaxed intergreat-power or interregional balance of power). An intergreat-power concert is correctly conceived and managed as substituting diplomatic for military and changing ad hoc for rigidly fixed coalitions, regrouping participants and reallocating their gains and losses in function of the momentarily salient issue. America functions as the concert's impartial conductor because it is qua fellow-player least directly involved in immediately contentious issues in Europe and flexibly engaged in a calculated realignment of priorities between Europe and Asia over an open-ended period of time.

Assumptions (and implicit policy preferences of the United States and other major and minor actors) behind this option and the alternative divide between Russia's disaggregation that continues the unraveling of its inner and outer empire and, conversely, the consolidation of the Russian Federation as a state that, while operating as an effective institutional and functional machinery, is also enshrouded in transcendent mystique. When this happens, great-power patriotism and updated religious orthodoxy replace beneficially a defunct ideology while amending successive deformations of a primitively prestatist czarist polity, absorbing prematurely an unworldly church, and the perversely creedal-statist Soviet regime—deformations rooted in deviation from the western European model of the evolutionary interlocks and sequences between church and state, state and society, and either state or society and the economy (wherein each first-named entity spawned the second-named only to be dispossessed by it as primary in due course). A Russia that has reconstituted itself as a state internally and functions as a great power externally (with sympathetic assistance of differently deviant America as a society grown out of flight from state-established church) presents the outside world, specifically the lesser powers at its periphery, with a related alternative and, consequently, policy option to be favored: those of a wide and of a narrow sphere of vital interests and influence. The former corrects for any prior imperial overextension by an altered style, the latter by the reduction of size, entailing a less thorough transformation of the preexisting empire form.

A large sphere includes and essentially hinges on parts of Europe west of Russia proper, while the defining gradation of style minimizes outright dominance closest to the core before passing through influence to nothing more than "presence" acknowledged as legitimate because operationally useful. The attendant intensity of involvement tapers off until the outermost margins of the Russian sphere meet and penetrate the sphere of an adjacent great power (Germany in Europe) or spheres of several such powers (in Asia)—and vice versa. The resulting interactions range from complementary to countervailing, but eschew open antagonisms, within an unequally relaxed balance-of-power setting and uneven degrees of the antecedent empire's or empires' progression from de-formalization to outright dissipation in interdependent relations between unequally powerful polities. Optimally, the gradation of actual or sought after influence along the axis from the inner to the outer zones of overlapping regional spheres and beyond improves on some of the risks and liabilities peculiar to a self-contained regional alliance "overextended" without sufficient reasons: to wit, the fact of gradation adjusts correspondingly the exposure of membership to the dilution of its value as well as uniformly operative dilution's inversion into discrimination implicit in assigning "forward" defense of the core to the most peripheral members. Unlike such peripherals, the marginals located within the overlap area of two spheres are not only not disqualified from performing their key role in the promotion of unification within the widest possible compass, but automatically contribute to integration.

Under this hypothesis, for the alternative of wide-and-overlapping spheres to become acceptable to the lesser states between Russia and Germany is in large part their responsibility, provided they are not driven to contrary courses by offers of momentarily attractive options more consistent with the alternative of Russia as a problem area. With respect to both the great and the lesser regional powers, the problem of overextension, fatal to empires in retrospective interpretation if not otherwise, fades as intergreat-power special relationships eliminate pressures for a preclusively expansionist response to qualitatively identical but operationally adverse adjacent powers at an empire's evolutionary midterm, an essentially defensive urge distinct from the predatory impulse directed at weak or chaotic forces that will have set off the initial expansion and will eventually inform offensively defensive protection of the imperial frontier from intrusive "uncivilized" forces. By the same token, the intergreat-power relationships perform overextension's positive function in that they minimize if not exclude the probability that an unoccupied space will be used against a power's (including Russia's) vital interests.

The lesser states located between Russia and Germany will respond to the option of a large but gradated Russian sphere positively or negatively depending on whether they have learned from the aftermath of the disintegration of another empire such as the Habsburg or Austro-Hungarian one, after 1918:

the geopolitics of divisively divergent responses to different regional greater powers perceived as most threatening (next to Germany for some, Italy and Soviet Russia for others) in conditions of economic dislocations (unevenly susceptible to remedies via trade, with Germany, or financial or other aid, from France) and internal ethno-cultural divisions between linguistic majorities and minorities.

After 1945, a supplementary factor of potential future significance concerns efforts at ideological and economic homogeneization of the successor states-to-be during the Soviet era. The question is whether the attempted uniformization has submerged ethnic and structural differences to at least some extent despite post-1989 appearances to the contrary. A part of a possible answer is implicit in the presently emerging alternative of the Polish-Hungarian and the Czech-Slovak model: the former spells regional re-homogeneization of sorts with help from coalitions including if not headed by left-wing or reformed-communist parties; the latter a re-polarization between a democratic-cum-capitalist western and a yet to be redefined and updated eastern type of political and economic regime. Provided that the former model delivers a sociopolitically less stressful economic transformation plus psychologically comforting feeling of national identity firm enough to sustain an evenhanded foreign policy toward West and East, it has an arguable amount of more widely applicable future-relevant pluses as opposed to the likewise discussable minuses of the latter model.

Reflecting residues from developments connected with both of the earlier starting dates, the post-1989 period exhibits an inconclusive drift toward alternative re-groupings within and beyond the ex-Habsburg space with unequally positive possible effects on the reorganization of ex-Soviet space.

A bifocally integrative centripetal model is intimated without being implemented in the Visegrad or a Visegrad plus grouping located geographically between Germany and Russia (and including the post-Habsburg countries as well as Ukraine and possibly the Baltic states from the post-Soviet complex). For such a grouping to perform its integrative function with respect to both of the great-power foci, it has to be consolidated by comparably calibrated functional and institutional links to both Germany and Russia and be firmed up ethno-culturally by parallel procedures: i.e., exchange Russia-friendly foreign policies of the smaller countries for Moscow's tolerance of less than ideal nationality policies toward Russian minorities and, symmetrically, purchase Bonn's and eventually Berlin's forbearance of "nationalistic" attitudes toward either the remaining German minorities or the compensation-seeking German expellees by a clear disposition to relate to unified Germany as not only the unavoidable but also actually preferred link to western Europe.

The contrasting model is divisively bipolar in structure and centrifugal in its effect on operations. As part of it some of the lesser countries (Czech Republic, Baltic states, and to a perhaps diminishing degree Hungary) practice a one-directional western orientation and others (prospectively Slovak Republic and presently Bulgaria and Belarus) are oriented eastward, while both place consequently a severe strain on prospects for the two-directional orientation of a third group (decreasingly independence-minded Ukraine and left-wing Poland and Hungary?) that might otherwise mediate betwen the two divergent orientations and, possibly, opposite models. This configuration is less likely than the alternative one to significantly contribute to a positive reorganization of ex-Soviet space and to a Russian foreign policy that implements its part in the formation of overlapping wide-and-gradated great power spheres.

The alternative to such a sphere is a small and comparatively exclusive sphere around a core power aimed at both an economic and a military-strategic monopoly of control. For Russia, Central Asia is the prime candidate for the position of such a constricted and up to a point constricting sphere compounding dominance with influence, to be consolidated (conformably with the type) in opposition to a range of alternative major-actor intruders intent on treating Central Asia as part of the larger ex-Soviet "problem area." In this context, the object of Russian (and any comparable power's) policy is to preempt competing influence with a view to translating exclusive access, maintained at an acceptable material cost, into an asset ensuring overall parity with a major competitor for regional role or global status—a critical difference from the large sphere option which entails a positive reconfiguration among actual or potentially "friendly" great powers with respect to structure and strategy. Within such a scheme, preemption is replaced with compensation and parity with a trade-off.

Specifically in the case of Russia, the compensation is for the "loss" of principally Ukraine and has the form of legitimation for expanded access to influence and presence in all of Europe. The corresponding trade-off is consequently between Russia's Europeanization (cum democratization) and renunciation of any future effort to reconstitute a Soviet- or Czarist-type empire including Ukraine and other "lost" parts of the inner and outer (East-Central European) empire. A large and gradated great-power sphere in the Western (including American) mode proceeds coincidentally with Western-style democratization in ways that defuse the predicaments implicit in a negative interplay, including real or hypothetical incompatibility, between democracy and empire. By contrast, confinement within the small Central Asian sphere is apt to stimulate differently compensatory expansion westward as an act of self-defense against integral Asianization, entailing authoritarian tendencies internally.

More inclusive than any particular interplays and associations is the comprehensive dialectic that would extract a positive Russian (and incidentally American) foreign policy from combining the two analytically counterposed kinds of spheres in ways that incidentally attenuate the divisive implications of the likewise ideal-typical alternative of the statist great-power and the pluralist problem area approach to Russia. The synthesis as prophecy or, beyond it, realistically utopian fantasy achieves plausibility when it replicates in terms of the Russo-German relationship for all of Europe what was already achieved for little Europe in the Franco-German relationship—an analogy that places Germany squarely in the center as not only the primary Central European power but more generally the key European power factor.

For France to offset Germany's demographic and economic advantage as a precondition of Franco-German complementarity in the formation of (Western) European community required its institutional leadership and nuclear-strategic capability within the "community" plus a token of world power status in the guise of France's postimperial sphere in Africa. Russia's equivalents are a plausible pretension to eventual diplomatic preeminence in all of Europe, sustained by a military-strategic capability usable for Europe's self-assertion abroad, and finally an extra-European position focused in and extending beyond Central Asia. As the indispensable complement to a repoliticized Germany's economic assets, realizing this Russian potential moves Europe past an economic to a geostrategically significant "power" while the attendant depolarization coincides with the relocation of Europe's center of gravity eastward. America's gradual disengagement from Europe, coinciding with the consensually accomplished crystallization of a gradated Russian sphere in consonance with Germany's, creates simultaneously the basis for a Russia saturated in Europe to join America wholeheartedly in a partnership displaced comparably eastward to Asia. This partnership, conceived and implemented so as not to provoke China as its putative target or alienate a Japan that perceives itself as marginalized (to a point exceeding the partly inescapable similar lot of France and Great Britain in Europe), becomes a key factor in a world order based on modified postempire regional spheres interrelated in a relaxed global balance of power.

A geopolitical scenario of future operations is significantly related to a meta- or macro-historical perspective in the subsoil of historicist intuition. The connection resides in the critical importance of the period separating a major continental power's first bid for hegemony from a second try, requiring two successive defeats for the would-be hegemon's subsequent liberalization. Sustaining attempts at a moderate domestic reform by successes in foreign policy could have avoided (post-Philip II Lerma era) Spain's, (post-Louis XIV

Choiseul etc. era) France's, and (post-Wilhelimine Weimar) Germany's slippage into the second bid. Russia presents a chance to avoid such a sequence through an approach to policy that interrogates history regarding Russia's present position on the prototypical trajectory of a major continental power without answering the query overconfidently with the postulate of the Soviet challenge having already been the second and decisively defeated bid (as opposed to the merely regional czarist contention with Britain not counting in the global perspective). Only when the "optimistic" interpretation is unconditionaly adhered to will reinforcing Russia's domestic liberalization with voluntarily conceded successes in foreign policy be unnecessary from the systemic (or geohistorical) perspective and, therefore, strategically redundant from the vantage point of an American phantom hegemony seen as endowed with a wholly exceptional mandate, immune to time and unabridgeable in space.

In light of a somewhat more realistically utopian fantasy, for the United States to freely concede postempire Russia's geopolitical Europeanization will help alleviate the adverse manifestations of America's own, sociopolitically prerevolutionary Europeanization. This beneficial congruence is but a special example of the primacy of geopolitics relative to economics. A provident grand strategy that implements this primacy relative to Russia will incidentally contain risks from hostile collisions between civilizations (in relation to China in particular). Moreover, efficient geopolitics renders the peculiar inner laws of economics manageable on both the intercivilizational and (relative to the Fourth World type of issues) the more comprehensive two-cities plane. Finally, channeling the processes of economics by means peculiar to geopolitics, which has the advantage of being more easily shaped than the processes by deliberate policies, will both augment the chances and control the side-effects of an expanding materialism absorbing ethno-cultural pseudo-idealisms (including those affecting modern Islam).

A complementary U.S.-Russian approach to different forms of Europeanization is not only a special but also a salient illustration of the operation of the key (geopolitical-economic-ethno-cultural) triangle, this functionally diffuse post-Cold War substitute for the geostrategically more focused U.S.-Soviet-Chinese triangle. Within it, a genuinely grand American strategy is the missing link between America's pervasive economism and occasional militarism as the discrete and individually insufficient approaches to crises either fostered or merely aggravated by nascent or reemergent nationalisms. This missing link is being forged only when U.S. policy moves beyond containment of the Soviet Union to the compensation of Russia for the abandonment of the Soviet empire, proceeding by way of the substitution of politic disengagement for military deterrence. If and when this happens, a truly new world order replaces an irretrievably missed occasion for a co-imperial pax with an even more decentralized but qualitatively superior postimperial peace. Based on a statism that is sufficiently normative to constrain chaotic pluralism and inject spirit into communitarian pluralism, such a peace celebrates a remarriage of high foreign with low domestic politics that releases global economy—as well as all kinds of novel technologies—from the lastingly unbearable burden of self-sufficiency attributed to either of the more "concrete" factors by a cultural predilection contrary to evidence assembled by history.

Notes

1. On the imperial option see in particular *The New Statecraft* (Chicago, IL: The University of Chicago Press, 1960), *Imperial America* (Baltimore, MD: The Johns Hopkins University Press, 1967), and *Career of Empire* (Baltimore, MD: The Johns Hopkins University Press, 1978); on the condominial option especially *Russia and the Road to Appeasement* (Baltimore, MD: The Johns Hopkins University Press, 1982) and *Rethinking U.S.-Soviet Relations* (Oxford, UK: Basil Blackwell, 1987). On the sequelae to the two options, *Return to the Heartland & Rebirth of the Old Order* (Washington, DC: The Johns Hopkins Foreign Policy Institute, 1994).

2. The *Washington Post*. In order of appearance arranged alphabetically, Charles Krauthammer ("Defining Success in the Balkans") and Stephen S. Rosenfeld ("Allied, Like It or Not") on December 8th, p. A 27; on December 10th, Charles Paul Freund ("Rhetoric on the Road to Tuzla") and Nicholas von Hoffman ("Like It or Not, We're and Empire"), p. C1, and Henry Kissinger ("Bosnia: Reasons for Care"), p. C9.

3. Cf. Francis Fukuyama, "The End of History?," *National Interest* (Summer 1989), pp. 3–18.

4. Cf. Samuel P. Huntington "Clash of Civilizations?," *Foreign Affairs* (Summer 1993), pp. 22–49.

5. The delineation of China's triad has been adapted from an unpublished survey of current interpretative trends in the China field by my Hopkins colleague Lyman Miller entitled "China's Long Revolution" (December 14, 1994). The observations on relationships between culture and policy in the Middle Kingdom are based on Arthur Waldron, *The Great Wall: From History to Myth* (Cambridge, UK: Cambridge University Press, 1990), ch. 10.

6. The essentially diplomatic implications of the United States as a "European Power" are discussed in Richard Holbrooke, "America, A European Power," *Foreign Affairs* (March/April 1995), pp. 38–51.

7. See Stephen S. Rosenfeld "Gingrich at the Water's Edge," *Washington Post*, July 21, 1995, p. A21, analyzing the Speaker's maiden foreign-policy speech before the Center for Strategic and International Studies.

8. Cf. Fukuyama, "The End of History?" and Huntington, "Clash of Civilizations?"

Index

America's contract with self and the world, precepts and propositions of, 60, 69, 74; premises and stipulations of, 69–75; purposes of, 84

Baltic countries, and European security and order, 17, 120
barbarians, definition of relative to civilization, 35; and global crisis, 39
Bosnian civil war, contending parties to, 23, 25, 30, 31–32; and Palestine, 44; procedural approaches to, 25–27, 42; substantive issues in, 24–25, 44; as symptom of wider pathologies, 23, 30; terms of settlement of, 27, 29

Central Asia, as Russian sphere of influence, 117, 121, 122
China, alternative foreign policies of, 14–15; and barbarians, 21; and European security, 18; Europe's discovery of, 10; facets in development of, 13–14; and multiculturalism, 56; as potential future hegemon, 80–81; relations with the West, 10, 13–14, 15, 20, 123; and Russia, 13, 15, 59, 81, 116, 118
civil society, conditions of globalization of, 45, 74, 102; as "open" society, 105
civilizations, aspects of, 11, 102; "clash" between, 10, 16, 36, 37, 54, 74, 89, 109–10, 123; vs. cultures, 11, 102; and history, 87–88, 102, 115. *See also* culture and cultures
class war, global, 36, 72, 83
co-guarantee, role in security architecture of, 18–19, 81
Cold War, aftermath of, 5, 20–21; essential character of, 33, 94; strategies associated with, 40–42, 57, 64, 72, 94
Commonwealth of Independent States (CIS); and NATO, 18
compensation; vs. containment as U.S. strategy toward Russia, 121, 123
conservatism; application to international relations of, 58–59; vs. liberalism, 62, 66, 92, 103; and postrevolutionary restoration, 56; social concerns of, 78, 103; types of, 63, 78, 90–91; and U.S. foreign policy, 59, 73
containment strategy; vs. compensation strategy, 121, 123; present modifications of, 42–43, 57
continental (Eurasian) arena and politics; and balance of power, 20; vs. insular-oceanic arena and politics, 12, 20, 62, 67; security structures and strategies for, 18, 81; and South-North issues, 64
"Contract with America", needed revisions of, 5–6, 7, 62; relevance for foreign policy of, 4

128   Index

crises. *See* domestic crises; global crises
Croats and Croatia. *See* Bosnian civil war
culture and cultures, American, 32, 61; vs. civilization and civilizations, 11, 21, 33, 61–62; dilution of, 61, 94, 96; and technological revolutions, 102. *See also* civilizations
Czech Republic. *See* East-Central Europe

defense, and discriminatory "forward" defense, 119; types of, 16, 41, 42, 84
deterrence, direct vs. indirect, 40, 41
devolution, and regional deconcentration, 108; as strategy on South-North type of issues, 41
disengagement, pre- and post-Cold War meanings of, 79–80; as a U.S. foreign policy, 42, 64, 108
domestic crises, reformist and revolutionary responses to, 44, 49, 70, 104–5; relation to global crises of, 47–49; in West generally and United States specifically, 37, 47, 48, 61, 96–97
Dulles, John Foster. *See* Eisenhower-Dulles "new look" strategy

East-Central Europe, alternative orientations of, 17, 19, 80, 107, 112; and Bosnian civil war, 31; and EU membership, 57; and NATO expansion, 31, 57, 80; relation to Western Europe, 60, 61, 78; representative governments in, 96; security options for, 17–18
East-West schism, connection with land-sea power schism of, 94; global manifestations of, 16, 111; intra-European manifestations of, 60, 61, 78, 94, 120
economic factor, vs. internal economy of politics, 56, 70; and interventionism, 67, 91–92; in peacemaking, 29–30; relative to domestic crises, 47–50; relative to population migrations, 41, 44–45, 47; role in world politics of, 78, 89–90, 91, 110–13, 123, 124; and varieties of economic determinism, 96; and (U.S.) informal free trade imperialism, 113
Eisenhower-Dulles "new look" strategy, present applicability of, 41, 42, 45, 59
empires. *See* great-power spheres; hegemony
equilibrium. *See* balance of power
ethical dilemmas, vs. moralism, 58, 70, 83, 84; and "politics of meaning," 97; and population migrations, 34, 43, 83, 98
ethno-cultural factor, and pseudo-idealism, 36, 45; relative to the geopolitical factor, 113, 123; relative to material deficiencies, 44, 45
Eurasia. *See* continental arena and politics
Europe, Americanization of, 51; conditions of renaissance, 97; as corporate power, 38, 94, 97; cultural dilution of, 94, 96; "little" vs. "greater," 13, 79, 95, 122; role of Eastern marginals in, 61, 95–96; two kinds of medievalism in, 87. *See also* European state system; U.S.-European relations
European state system, evolution of, 9, 10, 38, 71; U.S. effect on, 12, 85
European Union, and Bosnian civil war, 26; and coordination of foreign policies, 28; and Franco-German disparity, 95; "reason of state" deficit of, 97

Fourth World, and Eurasia 56; and new American contract with the world, 60; and "two cities of man," 48, 116. *See also* population migrations
France, 38; and Bosnian conflict, 23–24, 28, 30; and European state system, 12; parity with Germany of, 122; and World War I, 38

Germany, and Bosnian conflict, 23–24, 29; course in world politics of, 12, 38, 79; and East-Central Europe, 57, 80, 120; key role in Europe of, 122; and

Russia, 19, 20, 38, 91, 116, 117, 119, 122
global crises, and humanitarian palliatives, 44; kinds of, 20–21, 34, 37, 39, 43; relation to domestic crises, 48–49. *See also* domestic crises
Great Britain, as balancer and federalizer, 107–8; and Bosnian conflict, 28; empire of, 5; pre-World War I devolutionary strategy of, 79, 81, 91; and Russo-German accommodation, 91; "splendid isolation" of, 91; and World War I, 38
great-power spheres, indirect control in, 111, 112, 113; as informal empire substitutes, 110–11, 119; and intergreat-power concert, 118; overlaps between vs. overextension, 119; Russian vs. American, 117–18, 121; wide gradated vs. narrow constricting, 118–119, 121. *See also* hegemony
grand strategy, and "high" foreign politics, 56, 62, 65, 82, 116; main concerns of, 54, 56, 58, 73, 82, 92; negative vs. positive, 82, 84. *See also* statecraft
Gulf War, and "clash" of civilizations, 16; and economic factor, 49; and U.S. leadership, 30, 31

haves and have-nots, intra-Western and within U.S., 48, 50–51, 112. *See also* Fourth World; South-North axis and schism
hegemony, and American "statism," 103; and attendant dilemmas, 98, 102; vs. empire, 106–11, 112–13, 119; future candidates for, 80–81, 107, 108; vs. indirect control, 111; oriental version of, 109–10
"high" foreign politics, vs. formal diplomacy, 82, 101–2; vs. "low" politics, 56, 73, 82, 103–4, 116, 124. *See also* grand strategy
historicist intuition, application to world politics of, 106-24; vs. information and new type of knowledge, 51, 101; and metahistory, 122
history, and civilization, 87–88, 102, 115; continentalist vs. Anglo-Saxon version of, 37–38; continuities and change in, 10, 56, 62, 93; and neo- and post-phenomena, 92; presumptive end of, 10, 56, 88–89, 90, 102; returns to, 20, 36–37, 80, 86–88, 110; humanitarian intervention. *See* United Nations
human life, comparative valuation of, 32, 35
Hungary. *See* East-Central Europe

idealism, liberal and other, 36, 56, 58, 115; vs. materialism, 56, 83, 123; vs. realism, 55, 58, 82; and statism 56–57
insular-oceanic arena and politics, vs. continental arena and politics, 11, 12, 20, 62, 67, 90, 111, 117
Islam, and Bosnian conflict, 25, 26, 28; and "clash" of civilizations, 16, 123; and crusades, 10; and European security, 18; present condition of, 10; and Russia, 13, 21
isolationism, and American society, 50, 55, 103; vs. internationalism, 58, 114. *See also* liberal internationalism

Japan, and global security, 18; position and role in world affairs, 16, 20, 81, 116

Kennedy, John F., and liberal American empire, 2
Kissinger, Henry, and Nixon-Kissinger strategy, 2, 59, 107
Korean War, and the Eisenhower-Dulles "new look" strategy, 41

liberal internationalism, as aspect of decline, 112; conservative correction of, 45, 77; crisis of, 53; fading presuppositions of, 58–59, 70; and intervention-

ism, 67, 70; isolationist challenge to, 50, 78
Locarno Pact, eastern analogue of, 17–18, 80

Maginot Line, present equivalent of, 17, 21
materialism, as enemy of nationalism, 112; kinds of, 56–57; vs. naturalism, 70; and Western civilization, 74, 83
military factor, in contemporary international relations, 17, 45, 73, 90; and U.S. phantom hegemony, 31, 32, 114–15, 123
Muslims. See Bosnian civil war; Islam

"national interest", and American democracy, 114; as a problematic concept, 98; vs. systemic and civilizational interest, 38, 74, 78–79
nature and nurture. See political ecology
new world order, constituents of, 106–24; and postimperial (vs. co-imperial) peace, 124
Nixon-Kissinger strategy, 2, 107; and the Guam doctrine, 59
North Atlantic Free Trade Agreement (NAFTA), 54, 57
North Atlantic Treaty Organization (NATO), and China, 15, 108; and Commonwealth of Independent States, 18; and East-Central Europe, 17; expansion of, 19, 20, 31, 73, 80–81; and kinds of defense strategies, 16; obsolescence and reform of, 18, 54; and overextension, 119; role in Bosnia of, 1, 26; Senator Taft's alternative to, 59; and Russia, 18, 31, 108

Organization for Security and Cooperation in Europe (OSCE), and European security, 18

peacemaking and peacekeeping, in Bosnia, 26, 27, 31–2; generally, 29

pluralism, effect on foreign policies of, 55; institutionalized and chaotic, 10, 32; vs. statism, 62, 116–17. See also statism
Poland. See East-Central Europe
political ecology, as a nurture vs. nature issue, 43–44, 70, 72, 83–84, 88
population migrations, applicability of Cold War strategies to, 40–45; and intergreat-power relations, 64, 98; pathways and propellents of, 34, 37, 38; problems created by, 37, 47, 61; as threat to stability and cultural identity, 11, 20, 21, 34, 94
preventive diplomacy (and war), limitations of, 42
prophecy, vs. fantasy, 116; vs. prediction, 10, 33, 81–82; two prominent versions of, 10, 33, 81–82

realism, and American concretism, 114, 124; dialectical species of, 56, 58, 82, 115; and naturalism, 83
reform. See domestic crises; sociopolitical revolutions
regionalism, and balance of power, 54; economic variety of, 54, 57, 110; as evolutionary trend, 88, 90, 111–12; and former empires and dependents, 107–8, 112–13
Republican party, vs. Democratic party foreign policy strategies, 59–60
revolution. See sociopolitical revolutions; technological revolutions
Roman Empire, beleaguerment of, 20, 36–37; western and eastern successors to, 2, 9
Roosevelt, Theodore, and U.S. foreign policy, 5, 85
Russia, and alternative security architectures and strategies, 15, 16, 17, 18, 81; and America, 12, 15, 16, 65, 79, 117; and Bosnian conflict, 23–24, 26, 28, 31; and (Central) Asia, 79, 121, 122; and China, 13, 15, 20, 59, 65, 81,

Index   131

116, 117; democratization-cum-Europeanization of, 13, 20, 121; and East-Central Europe, 57, 80, 119–21; exposure to isolation of, 13; and Germany, 19, 20, 38, 91, 116, 117, 119, 122; historic role in European affairs of, 12; historic (autocracy-orthodoxy-nationality) trinity of, 13; and Islam, 13; multicultural society of, 56; and "near abroad," 20; and NATO, 18, 73; and population migrations, 21–22, 65; present evolutionary stage of, 122–23; as problem area vs. great power, 117, 121; and Weimar Germany, 16; and the West, 13, 21, 65, 79; wide vs. narrow interest spheres of, 118–19, 121
Rwanda, type of crisis in, 39, 41

security architectures and strategies, alternative forms of, 15, 16–17, 18–19, 59–60, 73; and the Locarno concept 17–18; vs. stability, 17–18
Serbs. *See* Bosnian civil war
siegecraft, relation to population migrations, 21–22, 34, 64, 116; vs. statecraft, 11, 21, 34–35, 57–58, 83
Slovak Republic. *See* East-Central Europe
social Darwinism, vs. international Wilsonism, 70–72; vs. Marxism-Leninism, 91; and naturalism in international relations, 70; reaffirmation against welfare statism of, 63, 86
society, distinguished from community, 35–36; relative to the state, 53–54, 66, 82, 102
sociopolitical ideologies, and foreign policies, 55; and information revolution, 51–52; and Western civilization, 86
sociopolitical revolutions, actual and pretended, 4, 62, 65, 71, 85; and "permanent prerevolution," 52; vs. reform, 104; and technological revolutions, 48, 52; and world politics, 7, 71. *See also* domestic crises

Somalia, type of crisis in, 39, 41
South-North axis and schism, vs. East-West schism, 19, 20, 21, 53, 57; and global haves and have-nots, 33, 36, 57, 82–83, 111; and political ecology, 43; strategic implications of, 40–45, 57; and the welfare state, 71. *See also* population migrations
space/time dimension, in world politics, 7, 106–7
stability, major threats to, 34, 39; vs. security and survival, 17, 40, 55, 109–10
state and state mystique, America's deficient sense of, 53–55, 66, 89; conservative view of, 63; demise of in Western Europe, 97; relationship to civilization of, 89; relationship to society of, 53, 54, 66, 82, 96, 102, 118; and "spirit," 89, 96; and war, 89–90
statecraft, contemporary role of, 17, 102; vs. siegecraft, 11, 21, 34, 64. *See also* grand strategy
state system, "passing" of in time and space, 36, 37
statism, and American hegemonism, 103; passing toward Asia of, 37; as a species of idealism, 56. *See also* pluralism

Taft, Robert A., and U.S. guarantee of European security, 59
technological revolutions, and global crises, 34; information- and knowledge-related, 48, 49–50, 52; vs. intuition and genuine knowledge, 51–52, 101–2; and political and wider culture, 102; and societal reform, 103; sociopolitical effects of, 48, 49–50, 51; and sociopolitical ideologies, 51–52; and U.S. foreign policy, 6, 7, 115; and world order, 124
totalitarianisms of Right and Left, and world politics, 9, 58, 71, 87
tragedy, vs. farce, 4, 115; role in world politics of, 3–4, 32, 34, 56, 115

triangle (post-U.S.-Soviet-Chinese), geopolitical-economic-ethno/cultural, 16, 113, 123
twentieth century, evaluation of, 92

Ukraine, and European security and order, 17, 120, 121
United Nations, humanitarian activities of, 4, 26, 30, 44, 83; and peacekeeping, 4, 41
United States, alternative security architectures and strategies for, 15, 16, 18, 81; and Bosnian conflict, 24–32; Byzantium-like characteristics of, 2, 115; and China, 6, 15, 16, 81, 107; contract with self and the world of, 63–66; domestic crises in, 47–52, 96–97; and empire, 5–6, 113-14; Europeanization of, 50–51, 104, 123; as a "European" power, 12, 19, 23, 37–38, 51, 60, 79–80, 81,91, 108; foreign vs. domestic politics of, 12, 84–85, 102–5, 114; informal free trade imperialism of, 113, 117; and NATO, 1, 18–19; as multicultural society, 56, 61–62, 68, 69; normative statist deficit of, 53–55, 58, 61, 63–64, 66, 74, 89, 102–3, 116; phantom hegemony of, 6–7, 30–31, 32, 63, 84, 102, 106, 113–15, 118, 123; political and mass culture of, 32, 78, 94, 103, 106; retrenchment requisite for, 12, 20, 57–58, 84-85; role in world politics of, 2–4, 5–6, 19, 23–24, 27, 31, 59–60, 63, 67–68, 74, 77, 85–86; and Russia, 12, 15, 117, 122–23; and Soviet Union 6, 15, 16, 81, 107; and tragedy, 4, 32, 98
U.S.-European relations, and America's new contract, 60–61, 74; and the Bosnian conflict, 28, 29; cultural dimension of, 78, 90; and decolonization, 38; Euro-Anglo/Saxon divergence in, 91; and the Russo-German connection 78–79. *See also* United States, Europe

values, expressed in "spirit," 89; deformations of, 58; and grand strategy, 58; role in world politics of, 55, 56, 66, 89; and tragic conflict 98
Vietnam War, and U.S. role in world affairs, 5, 31
Visegrad countries. *See* East-Central Europe

welfare state, challenge by social Darwinism to, 63, 84–85; costs of, 91–92; as counterutopia, 11, 71; exposure to "invisible hand" of, 47
the West, alternative scopes of, 19, 20; alternative security architectures for, 15; beleaguerment of, 11, 13, 15, 21, 59; immunities of, 39–40; and Russia, 13, 19, 79
Western civilization, and barbarians, 35; divisions within, 67; identity of, 33–34; imperilled ascendancy of, 9–10, 12-13, 65–66, 89; moralistic cultural imperialism of, 93; revitalization requisite of, 54, 74; and U.S. national interest, 98–99. *See also* civilizations; the West
Wilson, Woodrow, and U.S. foreign policy, 5, 62, 70, 85
world environment, crises inherent in, 20–21, 39, 53, 72; and determination of foreign policies, 55; normative vs. existential, 116; post-bipolar structure of, 20–21, 39, 43, 62, 98, 106
World War I, U.S. role in, 19, 37–38, 61, 69
World War II, place in history of, 5–6

Yugoslavia (former), type of crisis in, 39